Contents

Variance Analysis

E Harris and C West

The Chartered Institute of Management Accountants
63 Portland Place ▪ London ▪ W1N 4AB

Copyright © CIMA 1989, 1997

First published in 1989, revised 1997 by:

The Chartered Institute of Management Accountants

ISBN 1 874784 58 2

Chapter 1

Introduction

1.1   VARIANCE ANALYSIS, BUDGETS AND STANDARDS

Variance analysis

Variance analysis is an essential tool for effective management control. It is widely believed that costs can only be controlled through people.

It is people, in the form of responsible individuals, often managers, who have authority to control costs, who receive hourly, daily, weekly or monthly performance reports. These reports compare actual and budgeted performance and highlight the resulting variances.

The individuals are expected to respond to the variances reported. If the variances are adverse, the manager should first attempt to determine the cause of the variance and then ensure that it does not recur. If the variances are favourable, the manager should also attempt to determine the cause of the variance, which might be attributable to an easily achieved standard or a change in conditions. This may be an indication that the standard should be changed. However, if the variance is favourable, the manager should not be encouraged to adhere to the standard, but should be encouraged to repeat the performance.

Variance analysis – a definition

> The evaluation of performance by means of variances, whose timely reporting should maximise the opportunity for managerial action.

The difference between budgets and standards

All organisations can use budgets, whereas standard costing is most common in manufacturing organisations.

In broad terms a **budget** is a business plan for a future period of time, stated in financial terms. It is usually prepared in detail for the next financial year due to start shortly. It must be approved prior to the commencement of that period.

Budget – a definition

> A quantitative statement, for a defined period of time, which may include planned revenues, expenses, assets, liabilities and cash flows. A budget provides a focus for the organisation, aids the co-ordination of activities, and facilitates control. Planning is achieved by means of a fixed *master budget*, whereas control is generally exercised through the comparison of actual costs with a *flexible budget.*

Standard costs are costs which have been predetermined and are normally expressed on a per unit basis. In a manufacturing organisation, they are the costs which should be attained. They are the building blocks of budgets and help to evaluate performance and determine product costs.

Standard cost – a definition

> The planned unit cost of the products, components or services produced in a period. The standard cost may be determined on a number of bases. The main uses of standard costs are in performance measurement, control, stock valuation and in the establishment of selling prices.

Note

The terminology adopted in this book is that of *Management Accounting: Official Terminology* (Chartered Institute of Management Accountants, 1996), and relevant definitions from this appear in boxes in the text.

Figure 1.1: A chart of variances (using absorption costing)

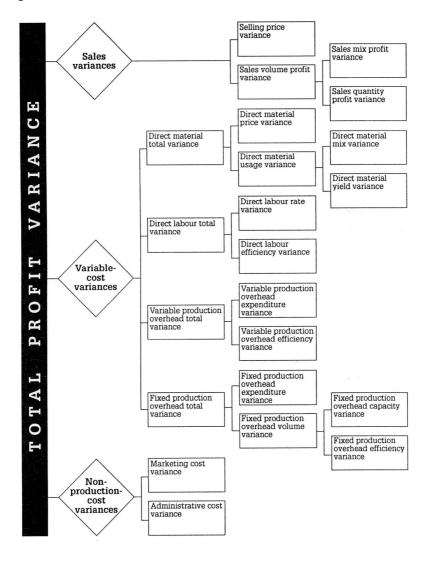

Figure 1.2: A chart of variances (using marginal costing)

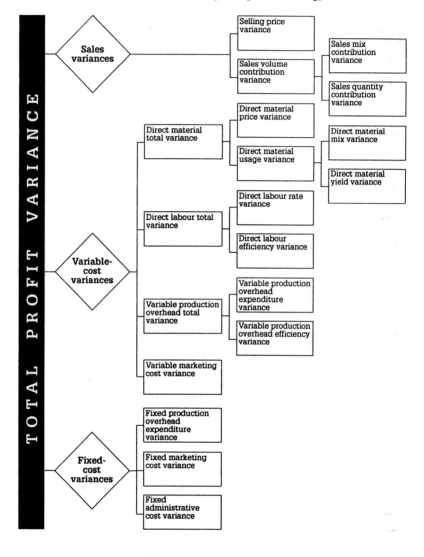

▓ Chapter 2

A simple illustration

2.1   THE PROBLEM

The following case study shows the normal procedures used to solve a simple variance analysis problem.

Plant Ltd

Plant Ltd is budgeting to make and sell 12,000 pumps per month in its new factory in Willenhall.

The following standards have been set by the management accountant:

	per unit
Direct material A	1.2 kg × £11 per kg
Direct material B	4.7 kg × £6 per kg
Direct labour	90 minutes at £8 per hour

Variable production overhead is absorbed at the rate of £10 per labour hour. Fixed production overhead is absorbed at the rate of £20 per labour hour.

Each pump is expected to be sold for £125.

The actual results for the month were:

Production and sales	12,600 units	
Material A	15,000 kg costing	£168,000
Material B	61,000 kg costing	£350,750
Direct labour	21,500 hours costing	£165,550
Variable production overhead		£214,240
Fixed production overhead		£372,000
Sales revenue		£1,549,800

During the month 900 labour hours were idle because of a leak from an overhead pipe. The operatives were paid in full for the idle time.

The factory manager would like to know whether the budgeted profit has been achieved. You have been asked to prepare an analysis of all relevant variances and to reconcile the actual profit with the budgeted profit for the month.

Solving the problem

Although the standards were set based on 12,000 pumps per month, the *actual level* of production was 12,600, an extra 600 pumps. It is not surprising that actual costs exceeded the budgeted costs. In variance analysis this is taken into account by *flexing* the budget or by calculating the *standard cost* of *actual production*. The *actual costs* are compared with the *budgeted costs* for the *actual level* of production.

	£
Actual cost of *actual* production	1,270,540
Standard cost of *actual* production	1,239,840
Total adverse production cost variance	
to be explained	**30,700**

The other part of the profit variance for the month is the effect that the different level of sales has had on the budgeted profit. An extra 600 pumps were produced, resulting in a higher level of costs, but as these additional 600 pumps were also sold, there will be a higher level of revenue and therefore of profit than originally budgeted.

The sales variances are calculated in terms of their effect on profit, *assuming costs are as standard*. It is very unlikely that the costs will be as standard, but any differences in costs will already be shown as *cost* variances and will not affect the evaluation of the *sales* variances.

2.2   STANDARD COSTS AND FLEXIBLE BUDGETS

The standard cost card

It is often helpful to prepare a standard cost card showing the standard costs for each element of cost per unit.

Standard costs per unit		£
Direct material A	1.2 kgs × £11 per kg	13.20
Direct material B	4.7 kgs × £6 per kg	28.20
Direct labour	90 min. × £8 per hour	12.00
Variable production overhead	90 min. × £10 per labour hour	15.00
Fixed production overhead	90 min. × £20 per labour hour	30.00
Total standard cost per unit		**98.40**

Detailed flexible budget

Having prepared the standard cost card it is then a relatively straightforward task to prepare a detailed flexible budget for the *actual* level of production based on these standard costs.

This is a vital step for each cost element, as the total variance is determined by comparing the actual cost with the flexible budget allowance.

Flexible budget for the actual level of production

Actual level of production   12,600 pumps
Standard costs for 12,600 pumps

		£
Direct material A	15,120 kg × £11 per kg	166,320
Direct material B	59,220 kg × £6 per kg	355,320
Direct labour	18,900 hours × £8 per hour	151,200
Variable production overhead	18,900 hours × £10 per labour hour	189,000
Fixed production overhead	18,900 hours × £20 per labour hour	378,000
Total standard cost		**1,239,840**

Note
The total standard cost can be checked as:

        12,600 pumps × £98.40 per pump, i.e. £1,239,840.

Actual results for the month

	£	£
Sales revenue		1,549,800
Costs:		
Material A	168,000	
Material B	350,750	
Direct labour	165,550	
Variable production overhead	214,240	
Fixed production overhead	372,000	
		1,270,540
Actual profit for the month		**279,260**

2.3   DESCRIBING THE VARIANCES

Favourable and adverse variances

The total production cost variance in section 2.1 was described as *adverse*, as the actual cost of production exceeded the standard cost allowed for production by £30,700. If the reverse had been the case and the actual cost of production had been less than the standard cost allowed, it would have been described as a *favourable* variance.

The terms 'adverse variances' and 'favourable variances' describe the effect on the *budgeted profit*. If the costs increase, the actual profit will be less than budgeted (an adverse variance). If the costs are reduced, the actual profit will be more than budgeted (a favourable variance). If the sales price or volume is increased, the actual profit will be more than budgeted (a favourable variance). If the sales price or volume is reduced, the actual profit will be less than budgeted (an adverse variance).

Chapter 3

Material variances

3.1 ANALYSING THE INFORMATION

In this example there are two materials. These are not considered to be inter-changeable. Chapter 10 covers material mix variances. Each material will be considered in turn.

Material A

It is helpful to follow a similar method to that used in Chapter 2 and to determine the direct material total variance to be explained. The *actual* costs are compared with the *standard* (or budgeted) costs for the *actual* level of production obtained from the flexible budget in section 2.2.

	£
Actual cost of Material A used	
15,000 kg × £11.20 per kg	168,000
Standard cost of Material A	
15,120 kg × £11 per kg	166,320
Direct material total variance	**1,680 (A)**

The variance is adverse (A) because the actual cost is greater than the standard cost.

Direct material total variance – a definition

> A measurement of the difference between the standard material cost of the output produced and the actual material cost incurred.
>
> Standard material cost of output produced – actual cost of material purchased
>
> Where the quantities of material purchased and used are different, the total variance should be calculated as the sum of the usage and price variances.

The direct material total variance is then further analysed to provide details of:

- how much of the change in cost is due to a change in the standard *price* of Material A.
- how much of the change in cost is due to a change in the standard *usage* of Material A.

There are a number of approaches to calculating the material *price* and *usage* variances. The simplest is to follow a logical format.

		£
MA1	*Actual* price of *actual* materials used	
	£11.20 × 15,000 kg	168,000
MA2	*Standard* price of *actual* materials used	
	£11 × 15,000 kg	165,000
MA3	*Standard* price of *standard* materials used	
	£11 × 15,120 kg	166,320

The direct material total variance is £1,680(A), the difference between lines MA1 and MA3.

The difference between MA1 and MA2 is the *price* variance, as it accounts for any change from the budgeted price of the materials used in production.

		£
MA1	15,000 kg – actual price £11.20 per kg	168,000
MA2	15,000 kg – standard price £11 per kg	165,000
	Direct material price variance	**3,000 (A)**

The variance is adverse (A) because the actual price paid per kg is higher than the standard (budgeted) price.

Direct material price variance – a definition

> The difference between the actual price paid for purchased materials and their standard cost.
>
> (actual quantity of material purchased × standard price)
>   – actual cost of material purchased

Note that this example calculates the material price variance based on the materials used. In practice the materials may be purchased in larger quantities and used over several months. An alternative method, basing the price variance on the materials purchased, is shown in chapter 9.

The difference between lines MA2 and MA3 is the *usage* variance, as it accounts for any change from the standard quantity of the materials used in production:

		£
MA2	15,000 actual kg × £11 per kg	165,000
MA3	15,120 standard kg × £11 per kg	166,320
	Direct material usage variance	1,320 (F)

The variance is favourable (F) because the actual usage is less than the standard usage.

Direct material usage variance – a definition

> Measures efficiency in the use of material, by comparing the standard cost of material used with the standard material cost of what has been produced.
>
> (actual production × standard material cost per unit)
>   – (actual material used × standard cost per unit)

You now have some information for the factory manager to explain why the actual cost of materials differed from the standard cost.

Summary of variances

	£
Direct material price variance	
15,000 kg × 20p per kg	3,000 (A)
Direct material usage variance	
120 kg × £11 per kg	1,320 (F)
Direct material total variance	**1,680 (A)**

Material B

It would be very helpful to attempt to calculate the price and usage variances for Material B using the format shown in section 3.1 for Material A and then to check the results with the information which follows. The *standard* costs are shown in the flexible budget in section 2.2.

	£
Actual cost of Material B	
61,000 kg × £5.75 per kg	350,750
Standard cost of Material B	
59,220 kg × £6 per kg	355,320
Direct material total variance	**4,570 (F)**

The variance is favourable (F) because the actual cost is greater than the standard cost.

To calculate the material *price* and *usage* variances, follow the logical format.

		£
MB1	*Actual* price of *actual* materials used	
	£5.75 × 61,000 kg	350,750
MB2	*Standard* price of *actual* materials used	
	£6 × 61,000 kg	366,000
MB3	*Standard* price of *standard* materials used	
	£6 × 59,220 kg	355,320

Price variance:

		£
MB1	61,000 kg – actual price £5.75 per kg	350,750
MB2	61,000 kg – standard price £6 per kg	366,000
	Direct material price variance	**15,250 (F)**

The variance is favourable (F) because the actual price paid per kg is lower than the standard (budgeted) price.

Usage variance:

		£
MB2	61,000 actual kg × £6 per kg	366,000
MB3	59,220 standard kg × £6 per kg	355,320
	Direct material usage variance	**10,680 (A)**

The variance is adverse (A) because the actual usage is greater than the standard usage.

Summary of variances

	£
Direct material price variance	
61,000 kg × 25p per kg	15,250 (F)
Direct material usage variance	
1,780 kg × £6 per kg	10,680 (A)
Direct material total variance	**4,570 (F)**

Methods of analysing the variances

In this book the same format will be used throughout. It is a reliable method and there are many similarities in the calculation of the material, labour and variable overhead variances. A more visual approach to the format is:

		Price		Quantity
M1		AP	×	AQ
	price/rate/expenditure variance			
M2		SP	×	AQ
	usage/efficiency variance			
M3		SP	×	SQ

Note that only one factor is varied when each variance is calculated.

3.2 EXPLAINING THE VARIANCES

Explanation of the material variances

The reasons for the material cost variances can now be given to the factory manager.

Material A

The materials were purchased at a price of £11.20 per kg which is 20p per kg higher than the standard price of £11 per kg. Overall, this cost £3,000.

However, the usage of materials was 120 kg less than expected, resulting in a saving of £1,320.

The reasons for the variances are not given, but it is possible that a higher-quality material was used, resulting in less wastage. Overall, the adverse variance was £1,680, so this would not be an advisable policy.

Material B

The materials were purchased at a price of £5.75 per kg, which is 25p per kg lower than the standard price of £6 per kg. This saved £15,250.

The usage of materials was 1,780 kg higher than expected, resulting in an additional cost of £10,680.

Again, the reasons for the variances have not been given. Assuming that a cheaper material was used, this resulted in a higher level of wastage than expected, but also resulted in an overall saving of £4,570. If this could be repeated, it would be cost-effective for the firm, assuming that there is no loss in the quality of the final product.

▓ Chapter 4

Labour variances

4.1   ANALYSING THE INFORMATION

Using the data

Using the data from Plant Ltd in section 2.1:

Actual production	12,600 pumps
Direct labour standards per unit	90 minutes
All direct operatives are paid at the	
rate of:	£8 per hour
Actual labour costs	21,500 hours costing £165,550

The analysis is very similar to that used for materials variances.

price variance	becomes	*rate* variance
usage variance	becomes	*efficiency* variance

Plant Ltd also involves calculating an *idle time* variance

Direct labour total variance – a definition

> Indicates the difference between the standard direct labour cost of the output which has been produced and the actual direct labour cost incurred.
>
> (standard hours produced × standard direct labour rate per hour)
>
>   – (actual hours paid × actual direct labour rate per hour)

The term *standard hour* needs some explanation. It is similar to the *standard quantity* of materials.

It is not unusual to talk of a 'three-hour journey' by car or train, even though traffic or weather conditions may make the journey shorter or longer than expected.

The decorating of a room could be described as a 'two-day job'. It is a useful concept to describe the quantity of work to be achieved.

With Plant Ltd the manufacture of 10 pumps would be a 'fifteen-hour job'. The standard hours required to produce 12,600 pumps would be 18,900 hours.

Standard hour – a definition

> The amount of work achievable, at standard efficiency levels, in an hour.

Note that a standard hour does *not* refer to time. It is a measure of output or production, which is achieved at normal efficiency levels.

The *standard hours* required to produce the actual 12,600 pumps have already been shown in section 2.2 in the detailed flexible budget:

18,900 standard hours at £8 per hour   £151,200

The standard hours are evaluated at the standard rate per hour to arrive at the standard labour cost of £151,200 for 12,600 pumps.

Calculating the variances

To determine the direct labour total variance, the *actual* costs are compared with the *standard* (or budgeted) costs for the *actual* level of production, from the flexible budget in section 2.2.

	£
Actual cost of labour hours paid	
21,500 hours × £7.70 per hour	165,550
Standard cost of standard labour hours	
18,900 hours × £8 per hour	151,200
Direct labour total variance	**14,350 (A)**

The variance is adverse (A) because the actual cost is greater than the standard cost.

Using a similar format as for material variances:

		£
L1	Actual rate for actual hours paid	
	£7.70 × 21,500 hours	165,550
L2	Standard rate for actual hours paid	
	£8 × 21,500 hours	172,000
L3	Standard rate for actual hours worked	
	£8 × 20,600 hours	164,800
L4	Standard rate for standard hours allowed	
	£8 × 18,900 hours	151,200

It is necessary to include an extra line, L2, as an extra variance needs to be calculated. The example stated that 900 labour hours were idle because of a leak from an overhead pipe, and that the operatives were paid in full for the idle time. The *idle time* variance is therefore 900 hours × £8 per hour = £7,200 (A). An idle time variance will *always* be adverse .

Idle time variance – a definition

The standard labour cost of unproductive paid hours, when production was not possible due to factors such as material unavailability, production planning errors or machine breakdown.

(actual hours paid × standard direct labour rate per hour)
      – (actual hours worked × standard direct labour rate per hour)

The direct labour total variance is £14,350 (A), the difference between L1 and L4.

The difference between L1 and L2 is the *rate* variance, as it accounts for any change from the standard (budgeted) rate of the labour hours paid.

		£
L1	21,500 hours × actual rate £7.70 per hour	165,550
L2	21,500 hours × standard rate £8 per hour	172,000
	Direct labour rate variance	**6,450 (F)**

The variance is favourable (F) because the actual rate paid is less than the standard (budgeted) rate.

Direct labour rate variance – a definition

> Indicates the actual cost of any change from the standard labour rate of remuneration.
>
> (actual hours paid × standard direct labour rate per hour)
> – (actual hours paid × actual direct labour rate per hour)

The difference between L2 and L3 is the *idle time* variance, as already calculated.

		£
L2	21,500 hours paid × £8 per hour	172,000
L3	20,600 hours worked × £8 per hour	164,800
	Direct labour idle time variance	7,200 (A)

The difference between L3 and L4 is the *efficiency* variance, as it accounts for any change from the standard hours required for production.

		£
L3	20,600 actual hours worked × £8 per hour	164,800
L4	18,900 standard hours allowed × £8 per hour	151,200
	Direct labour efficiency variance	13,600 (A)

The variance is adverse (A) because the actual hours worked are greater than the standard hours allowed.

Direct labour rate variance – a definition

> Indicates the standard labour cost of any change from the standard level of labour efficiency.
>
> (actual production in standard hours × standard direct labour rate per hour)
>
> – (actual direct labour hours worked × standard direct labour rate per hour)

Summary of variances

	£	
Direct labour rate variance	6,450	(F)
Direct labour idle time variance	7,200	(A)
Direct labour efficiency variance	13,600	(A)
Direct labour total variance	**14,350**	**(A)**

4.2 EXPLAINING THE VARIANCES

Explanation of the labour variances

The reasons for the labour cost variances can now be given to the factory manager.

All labour was paid at a rate 30p per hour less than the standard. It is possible that a lower grade of labour was used, perhaps because of a shortage of skilled labour.

The direct labour idle time variance was caused by a leak from an overhead pipe and meant that 900 unproductive labour hours were paid for, costing £7,200.

The direct labour efficiency variance arose as the work was intended to take 18,900 standard hours, but 20,600 hours were worked. It is possible that the extra time needed is a direct consequence of using a lower and less skilled grade of labour.

The net effect of the labour rate and efficiency variances, excluding idle time, is £7,150 (A). It would seem to be advisable to try to use labour of the correct grade for the manufacture of the pumps, in order to achieve the normal level of efficiency.

The real cost of idle time

If a factory is working at full capacity, then any loss of production through idle time will be a permanent loss. The same logic applies to the manufacture of any product with a very short life, such as a newspaper.

In these cases, the cost of idle time is not just the additional cost of unproductive labour time. The real cost will be the loss of contribution as a direct result of the loss of production.

This topic is covered in greater depth in Chapter 9.

Chapter 5

Variable production overhead variances

5.1   IDLE TIME AND ABSORPTION RATES

The treatment of idle time

The analysis of the variances is very similar to that used for labour variances, but with one exception, the idle time variance.

Overhead cost – a definition

> Expenditure on labour, materials or services which cannot be economically identified with a specific saleable cost unit.

At this stage it is *variable* production overhead which is being considered. A large proportion of the total variable overhead cost will be the power used in running the machinery. When the machinery is not being used for production, the power will be switched off and no variable production overhead costs will be incurred.

This is exactly what will happen during the direct labour idle time which resulted from the leaking overhead pipe. The machinery would not be running and therefore there is no variable production overhead idle time variance to be accounted for.

Variable production overhead and absorption rates

All production overhead costs, whether variable or fixed, are normally absorbed into the cost of production using a predetermined or budgeted rate. Variance analysis is no exception to this method.

Use the data from Plant Ltd in section 2.1.

Actual production	12,600 pumps
Variable overhead production costs	£214,240

It is important to identify the *number* of labour hours used to absorb the variable overhead production costs of £214,240. This must be based on the labour hours *worked*, excluding idle time. The data states that 21,500 hours were paid and that 900 hours were idle. Therefore the labour hours worked are 20,600 and this is also the number of hours used for evaluating the variable production overhead variances.

The analysis is very similar to that used for labour variances.

rate variance	becomes	*expenditure* variance
efficiency variance	remains	*efficiency* variance

5.2   ANALYSING THE INFORMATION

Calculating the variances

To determine the variable production overhead total variance, the *actual* costs are compared with the *standard* (or budgeted) costs for the *actual* level of production, using the flexible budget in section 2.2.

	£
Actual cost of variable production overhead	
20,600 hours × £10.40 per labour hour	214,240
Standard cost of standard labour hours	
18,900 hours × £10 per labour hour	189,000
Variable production overhead total variance	**25,240 (A)**

The variance is adverse (A) because the actual cost is greater than the standard cost.

Variable production overhead total variance – a definition

> The difference between the amount of variable production overhead which has been absorbed by output, and the actual cost.
>
> actual cost incurred – (actual production in standard hours ×
> variable production overhead absorption rate per hour)

Using a similar format as for material and labour variances:

		£
V1	Actual rate for actual hours worked	
	£10.40 × 20,600 hours	214,240
V2	Standard rate for actual hours worked	
	£10 × 20,600 hours	206,000
V3	Standard cost for standard hours allowed	
	£10 × 18,900 hours	189,000

The difference between V1 and V2 is the *expenditure* variance, as it accounts for any change from the standard (budgeted) rate of the labour hours (and therefore variable overhead hours) worked.

		£
V1	20,600 hours × actual rate £10.40 per hour	214,240
V2	20,600 hours × standard rate £10 per hour	206,000
	Variable production overhead expenditure variance	**8,240** (A)

The variance is adverse (A) because the actual rate paid is greater than the standard (budgeted) rate.

Variable production overhead expenditure variance – a definition

> Measures the difference between the actual variable production overhead costs and those in a budget flexed on labour hours.
>
> actual cost incurred – (actual hours worked × standard variable production overhead absorption rate per hour)

The difference between V2 and V3 is the *efficiency* variance, as it accounts for any change from the standard hours required for production.

		£
V2	20,600 actual hours × £10 per hour	206,000
V3	18,900 standard hours × £10 per hour	189,000
	Variable production overhead efficiency variance	**17,000** (A)

The variance is adverse (A) because the actual hours worked are greater than the standard hours allowed.

Note that the 1,700 hours which represent the efficiency variance (20,600 actual hours less 18,900 standard hours) is exactly the same number of hours which represented the efficiency variance when calculating the labour variances.

In the labour variances, the efficiency variance is evaluated as 1,700 hours at the labour rate of £8 per hour, i.e. £13,600 (A). In the variable production overhead variances, the efficiency variance is evaluated as 1,700 hours at the variable production overhead rate of £10 per hour, i.e. £17,000 (A).

Even when there is an idle time variance, the *efficiency* variance in labour and variable production overhead will always be represented by the same number of hours.

Variable production overhead efficiency variance – a definition

> Measures the difference between the variable overhead cost budget flexed on actual labour hours and the variable overhead cost absorbed by output produced.
>
> (actual hours worked × standard variable production overhead absorption rate per hour) – (actual production in standard hours × variable absorption rate per hour)

Summary of variances

	£
Variable production overhead expenditure variance	8,240 (A)
Variable production overhead efficiency variance	17,000 (A)
Variable production overhead total variance	**25,240 (A)**

5.3   EXPLAINING THE VARIANCES

Explanation of the variable production overhead variances
The reasons for the variable production overhead variances can now be given to the factory manager.

The actual variable production overhead averaged out at a cost of

£10.40 per hour. No reason has been given for this increase, but it is possible that, as the pumps are being produced in a new factory, it was difficult to predict accurately the budgeted variable production overhead rate per hour.

The variable production overhead efficiency variance is a direct result of the labour efficiency variance. It was suggested in section 4.2 that the use of low grade and less efficient labour was not cost-effective. If the added cost of running machinery for an extra 1,700 hours is included as a cost of labour inefficiency, then this variance becomes £24,150 (A).

	£
Labour rate variance	6,450 (F)
Labour efficiency variance	13,600 (A)
Variable production overhead efficiency variance	17,000 (A)
Total effect of labour variances	**24,150 (A)**

Presenting the variances in this manner would highlight the true cost of labour inefficiency, for whatever reason.

The real cost of the labour efficiency variance

In section 4.2 it was suggested that the real cost of idle time can be much higher than the labour idle time variance if a factory is working at full capacity. The same logic can be applied to the labour efficiency variance.

If the budgeted production cannot be produced in full because of an adverse labour efficiency variance, then any loss of production will be a permanent loss. The real cost is the lost contribution as a direct result of the loss of production.

Conversely, if the budgeted production is exceeded because of a favourable labour efficiency variance, the additional production will be sold and the real benefit will be measured by the additional contribution as a direct result of the increased production.

Again, this topic is covered in greater depth in Chapter 9.

Chapter 6

Fixed production overhead variances

6.1 ABSORPTION RATES AND FIXED PRODUCTION OVERHEAD

Fixed production overhead absorption rates

All production overhead costs are normally absorbed into the cost of production using a predetermined or budgeted rate.

There are two possible ways of absorbing overhead costs into production:

1. Assuming *budgeted* production overhead costs are absorbed on the basis of the *budgeted level of production, in units.*
2. Assuming *budgeted* production overhead costs are absorbed on the basis of the *budgeted hours.*

Refer back to the chart of variances shown in Figure 1.1. The simplest method is the first method, which results in only an *expenditure* and a *volume* variance.

A slightly more complex method involves the further analysis of the *volume* variance into an *efficiency* variance and a *capacity* variance.

There is normally no choice as to which method is to be used. If there is any indication that production overheads are absorbed on the basis of budgeted hours, then the second, more complex method must be used.

6.2 VARIANCE CALCULATIONS ASSUMING ABSORPTION IS BASED ON UNITS OF PRODUCTION

Assuming that production overhead is absorbed on the basis of budgeted units

Firstly, determine the budgeted fixed production overhead data.

Using the data from Plant Ltd in section 2.1:

Budgeted production	12,000 pumps
Budgeted fixed overhead absorption rate	£20 per hour

As the standard time allowed for each pump is 90 minutes, then the budgeted fixed overhead absorption rate per pump is £30 and the original total *budgeted* fixed production overhead cost must be £360,000 (12,000 pumps × £30 per pump). It is essential to calculate the total budgeted fixed production overhead in order to determine the expenditure variance.

The names of the variances are similar to those used for labour variances, but the methods of calculation differ slightly.

Calculating the variances assuming absorption is on the basis of budgeted units

To determine the fixed production overhead total variance, the actual costs are compared with the fixed production overhead costs absorbed, obtained from the flexible budget in section 2.2.

	£
Actual cost of fixed production overhead	372,000
Standard cost of fixed production overhead	
12,600 units × £30 per unit	378,000
Fixed production overhead total variance	**6,000 (F)**

The variance is favourable (F) because the actual cost is less than the standard cost.

Fixed production overhead total variance – a definition

The difference between the actual fixed production overhead incurred and the amount absorbed by output produced. This is the sum of the expenditure and volume variances.

(actual production in standard hours × fixed production overhead absorption rate per hour) – actual fixed production overhead

Using a similar format as for variable overhead variances:

		£
F1	*Actual* cost of fixed production overhead	372,000
F2	*Budgeted* cost of fixed production overhead	
	12,000 units × £30 per unit	360,000
F3	*Standard* cost of fixed production overhead	
	12,600 units × £30 per unit	378,000

Note that F2 represents the *budgeted* cost of fixed production overhead and is *completely* different from the methods used to calculate material, labour and variable overhead variances.

The difference between F1 and F2 is the *expenditure* variance, as it accounts for any change from the original budgeted fixed production overhead cost.

		£
F1	Actual cost of fixed production overhead	372,000
F2	Budgeted cost of fixed production overhead	
	12,000 units × £30 per unit	360,000
	Fixed production overhead expenditure variance	**12,000 (A)**

The variance is adverse (A) because the actual cost of the fixed production overhead is greater than the budgeted amount. Fixed production overhead costs are considered *not* to vary with the level of production, so any variation from the budgeted cost is named an *expenditure* variance.

Fixed production overhead expenditure variance – a definition

> The difference between the fixed production overhead which should have been incurred in the period, and that which was incurred.
>
> budgeted fixed production overhead – actual fixed production overhead

The difference between F2 and F3 is the *volume* variance as it accounts for any change in the volume (quantity) of production from the *budgeted* level.

		£
F2	Budgeted cost of fixed production overhead	360,000
	12,000 units × £30 per unit	
F3	Standard cost of fixed production overhead	378,000
	12,600 units × £30 per unit	
	Fixed production overhead volume variance	**18,000 (F)**

The *volume* variance represents the over- or underabsorption of fixed production overhead as the *actual* level of production differed from the *budgeted* level of production. It is favourable (F) for two reasons. Firstly, more pumps were produced than budgeted. Assuming that these can be sold, then the profit will increase. Secondly, the fixed production overhead has been *overabsorbed* as 600 additional pumps were produced and therefore the cost of production has been overstated by 600 × £30, i.e. £18,000. The favourable variance shows that there should be a reduction in the fixed production overhead element of the cost of production, which is currently assumed to be £378,000.

Fixed production overhead volume variance – a definition

> A measure of the over- or underabsorption of overhead cost caused by actual production volume differing from that budgeted.
>
> (actual production in standard hours × fixed production overhead absorption rate per hour) – budgeted fixed production overhead

Note that although the *Official Terminology* refers to the volume variance in terms of the fixed production overhead absorption rate *per hour*, this variance is much easier to calculate when considered in terms of the fixed overhead absorption rate *per unit*.

Summary of variances

	£
Fixed production overhead expenditure variance	12,000 (A)
Fixed production overhead volume variance	18,000 (F)
Fixed production overhead total variance	**6,000 (F)**

Explanation of the fixed production overhead variances

This has already been discussed in the course of calculating the variances.

The fixed production overhead expenditure was £12,000 more than budgeted. It would be quite wrong to suggest that this was caused by the production of an additional 600 pumps. The nature of fixed production overhead costs is that they do not vary with the level of output. It is possible that, as for the variable overhead expenditure variance, it was difficult to predict accurately the budgeted fixed production overhead for the period.

The fixed production overhead volume variance simply represents the overabsorption of fixed production overhead costs as actual production exceeded the budgeted level by 600 pumps.

Effect on variable overhead variances of assuming budgeted production overhead costs are absorbed on the basis of the budgeted level of production

If fixed and variable production overheads are absorbed on the basis of a rate per unit, rather than a rate per hour, then there is no concept of *standard* hours for overheads and therefore there can be no *efficiency* variance.

In this case, the calculation of the variable production variances becomes much simpler and the only variance to be calculated is the expenditure variance.

		£
V1	Actual cost of variable production overhead	214,240
V2	Standard cost of variable production overhead	
	12,600 units × £15 per unit	189,000
	Variable production overhead expenditure	
	variance	**25,240 (A)**

The variable production overhead efficiency variance is not calculated as there can be no comparison of standard hours or actual hours.

Variable production overhead expenditure variance – a definition

> If variable production overheads vary with output, rather than with hours worked, the variance would be calculated as follows.
>
> actual cost incurred – (output produced × variable production overhead rate per unit produced)

Variable production overhead total variance – a definition

> Where variable production overhead varies with output, this is identical to the variable production overhead expenditure variance.

6.3 VARIANCE ANALYSIS ASSUMING ABSORPTION IS BASED ON HOURS OF PRODUCTION

Assuming that production overhead is absorbed on the basis of budgeted hours

Firstly, determine the budgeted fixed overhead data.

Use the data from Plant Ltd in section 2.1.

Budgeted production	12,000 pumps
Budgeted fixed production overhead absorption rate	£20 per hour

As the standard time allowed for each pump is 90 minutes, then the total *budgeted* fixed production cost is £360,000. It is essential to calculate the total budgeted fixed production overhead in order to determine the expenditure variance.

The chart of variances from Figure 1.1 may be helpful at this point.

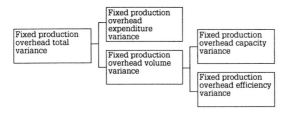

The expenditure variance remains the same as given in section 6.2 but the volume variance must be further analysed into an efficiency variance (similar to labour and variable overhead efficiency variances) and a capacity variance.

Calculating the variances assuming absorption is on the basis of budgeted hours

The fixed production overhead total variance is determined, as in section 6.2, by comparing the actual costs with the fixed production overhead costs absorbed at the budgeted rate per hour (from the flexible budget in section 2.2).

	£
Actual cost of fixed production overhead	372,000
Standard cost of fixed production overhead	
(18,900 hours × £20 per labour hour)	378,000
Fixed production overhead total variance	**6,000 (F)**

The variance is favourable (F) because the actual cost is less than the standard cost.

Varying the format slightly:

		£
FO1	Actual cost of fixed production overhead	
	20,600 hours	372,000
FO2	Budgeted cost of fixed production overhead	
	18,000 hours × £20 per hour	360,000
FO3	Actual hours worked at standard rate	
	20,600 hours × £20 per hour	412,000
FO4	Standard hours at standard rate	
	18,900 hours × £20 per hour	378,000

As before, the difference between FO1 and FO2 is the *expenditure* variance, as it accounts for any change from the budgeted fixed production overhead cost.

		£
FO1	Actual cost of fixed production overhead	372,000
FO2	Budgeted cost of fixed production overhead	
	18,000 hours × £20 per hour	360,000
Fixed production overhead expenditure variance		**12,000 (A)**

The difference between FO2 and FO3 is the *capacity* variance, as it accounts for any change from the *budgeted* capacity (as measured in hours worked).

		£
FO2	Budgeted cost of fixed production overhead	
	18,000 hours × £20 per hour	360,000
FO3	Actual hours worked at standard rate	
	20,600 hours × £20 per hour	412,000
Fixed production overhead capacity variance		**52,000 (F)**

The *capacity* variance represents the over- or underabsorption of fixed production overhead as the *actual* number of hours worked differed from the *budgeted* hours. It is favourable (F) for two reasons. Firstly, more hours were worked than budgeted. Assuming that this results in additional production and sales, then the profit will increase. Secondly, the fixed production overhead has been *overabsorbed* as an additional 2,600 hours were worked in excess of the budget, and therefore the cost of production has been overstated by 2,600 × £20, i.e. £52,000. The favourable variance shows that there should be a reduction in the fixed production overhead element of the cost of production, which is currently assumed to be £412,000.

Fixed production overhead capacity variance – a definition

Measures the over- or underabsorption of fixed production overhead costs caused by the actual hours worked differing from the hours originally budgeted to be worked. A subdivision of the fixed production overhead volume variance.

(actual hours worked × standard fixed production overhead absorption rate per hour) − (budgeted hours to be worked × standard fixed production overhead absorption rate per hour)

The difference between FO3 and FO4 is the *efficiency* variance. This is calculated in exactly the same way as the efficiency variance for labour and variable overhead costs and is represented by 1,700 hours, exactly the same number of hours, as it accounts for any change from the standard hours required for production.

		£
FO3	Actual hours worked at standard rate	
	20,600 hours × £20 per hour	412,000
FO4	Standard hours at standard rate	
	18,900 hours × £20 per hour	378,000
	Fixed production overhead efficiency variance	**34,000 (A)**

The variance is adverse (A) because the actual hours worked are greater than the standard hours allowed.

In the labour variances, the efficiency variance is calculated as 1,700 hours at the labour rate of £8 per hour, i.e. £13,600 (A). In the variable production overhead variances the efficiency variance is evaluated as 1,700 hours at the variable production overhead rate of £10 per hour, i.e. £17,000 (A). In the fixed production overhead variances the efficiency variance is evaluated as 1,700 hours at the fixed production overhead rate of £20 per hour, i.e. £34,000 (A).

Fixed production overhead efficiency variance – a definition

> Measures the over- or underabsorption of fixed production overhead costs caused by actual labour efficiency differing from the standard level of labour efficiency. A subdivision of the fixed production overhead volume variance.
>
> (actual hours worked × standard fixed production overhead absorption rate per hour) – (actual production in standard hours × fixed production overhead absorption rate per hour)

Summary of variances

	£
Fixed production overhead expenditure variance	12,000 (A)
Fixed production overhead capacity variance	52,000 (F)
Fixed production overhead efficiency variance	34,000 (A)
Fixed production overhead total variance	6,000 (F)

Note that the capacity and efficiency variances net off to equate to the total volume variance.

	£
Fixed production overhead capacity variance	52,000 (F)
Fixed production overhead efficiency variance	34,000 (A)
Fixed production overhead volume variance	18,000 (F)

Explanation of the fixed production overhead variances

This has already been discussed in the course of calculating the variances.

The fixed production overhead expenditure was £12,000 more than budgeted. This cannot be attributed to the production of an additional 600 pumps. It is possible that it arose because of the difficulty in predicting accurately the budgeted fixed production overhead for the period in the new factory.

The fixed production overhead capacity variance represents the overabsorption of fixed production overhead cost as actual hours worked exceeded the budgeted level by 2,600 hours.

The fixed production overhead efficiency variance represents the fact that the actual hours worked exceeded the standard hours allowed by 1,700 hours. Both the capacity and efficiency variances are evaluated at the budgeted absorption rate per hour.

Chapter 7

Sales variances

7.1 SALES VARIANCES AND PRODUCTION OVERHEAD VARIANCES

Sales variances and fixed production overhead variances

When absorption costing is used, the calculation of the *sales volume* variance is very similar to that of the *fixed production overhead volume variance*.

When there is no change in finished goods stock levels and therefore production and sales are equal, the number of *units* represented by the *fixed production overhead volume variance* will be identical to the number of *units* represented by the *sales volume variance*.

7.2 SALES VARIANCES AND PROFIT

Sales variances and their effect on profit

All the cost variances in Chapters 3–6 have been calculated in terms of their effect on the budgeted *profit*. An adverse variance of £1,500 increases costs by £1,500 and *reduces profit* by £1,500. Conversely, a favourable variance of £800 reduces costs by £800 and *increases profit* by £800.

The sales variances must be calculated in exactly the same way – in terms of their effect on profit.

The sales price variance will automatically be calculated in this way. A reduction of £2 in the price per unit directly reduces profit by £2 for each unit sold. Conversely, an increase of £3 in the price per unit directly increases profit by £3 per unit.

Sales variances are always calculated assuming that costs will be standard. If the costs are *not* standard, as in most cases, then any variances are separately analysed as *cost variances*, materials, labour, variable or fixed production overhead variances.

The sales volume variance could be calculated in terms of its effect on sales revenue, but this will not be helpful information for the factory manager. It must always be calculated in terms of its effect on the budgeted profit. The sales volume variance must always be evaluated at the *standard profit per unit* when absorption costing is used.

The analysis is very similar to that used for fixed production overhead variances.

Expenditure variance	becomes	*price* variance
Volume variance	remains	*volume* variance

7.3 ANALYSING THE INFORMATION

Using the data

Use the data from Plant Ltd in section 2.1.

Budgeted selling price	£125
Budgeted production and sales	12,000 pumps
Actual production and sales	12,600 pumps
Sales revenue	£1,549,800

The actual selling price can be calculated as:

$$\frac{£1,549,800}{12,600 \text{ units}} = £123 \text{ per pump}$$

Calculating the variances

It is not easy to determine the sales total variance, as the most obvious calculation will result in the total change in *sales revenue*, rather than showing the effect on budgeted *profit* of changes in the sales price and volume. For this reason it is not recommended.

Sales price variance – a definition

> The change in revenue caused by the actual selling price differing from that budgeted.
>
> (actual sales volume × standard selling price per unit) – actual sales revenue

The previous format is not very useful for the sales price variance, but an adaptation can be used.

		£
S1	*Actual* selling price of *actual* sales volume	
	£123 × 12,600 units	1,549,800
S2	*Standard* selling price of *actual* sales volume	
	£125 × 12,600 units	1,575,000
	Sales price variance	**25,200 (A)**

Note that this variance is automatically calculated in terms of its effect on profit, as any change in selling price has a direct effect on profit.

The variance is adverse (A) as each pump was sold for £2 less than the budgeted price.

The sales volume variance is calculated in an identical manner to the fixed overhead volume variance, but evaluated at the standard *profit* per unit. The standard profit per unit is calculated using the budgeted selling price of £125 and the total standard cost per unit from section 2.2 of £98.40 per unit.

The standard profit is:

	£
Standard selling price	125.00
Standard cost per unit	98.40
Standard profit per unit	**26.60**

Sales volume profit variance – a definition

> The change in profit caused by sales volume differing from that budgeted.
>
> (budgeted sales × standard profit per unit) – (actual sales × standard profit
>
> per unit)

		£
S3	Actual sales × standard profit per unit	
	12,600 × £26.60	335,160
S4	Budgeted sales × standard profit per unit	
	12,000 × £26.60	319,200
	Sales volume profit variance	**15,960 (F)**

Note that sales variances are *favourable* when the 'actual' is greater than the 'standard' or 'budget' and are *adverse* when the 'actual' is less than the 'standard' or 'budget'. This is the reverse of the cost variances.

7.4 EXPLAINING THE VARIANCES

Explanation of the sales variances

The sales price variance represents the reduction in profit as a result of selling the pumps at £2 per unit less than the budgeted price of £125. As 12,600 pumps were sold, the loss of revenue is evaluated as 12,600 × £2 = £25,200 (A).

The sales volume variance represents the additional 600 pumps which were sold, evaluated at the standard profit of £26.60 per pump, a total of £15,960 (F).

If there was a deliberate policy to increase the overall profit by reducing the price per pump in order to sell additional pumps, it was not beneficial, as the overall effect on profit was £9,240 (A).

	£
Sales price variance	25,200 (A)
Sales volume (profit) variance	15,960 (F)
Total effect on profit	**9,240 (A)**

However, if the reduction in price was a reaction to competitors' price reductions, then the policy may have been beneficial, as the volume of sales increased by 5 per cent. If the selling price had remained at £125, it is likely that there would have been a considerable reduction in the sales volume in the same circumstances.

Chapter 8

Reconciliation of budgeted and actual profit

8.1   TWO DIFFERENT APPROACHES

The reconciliation statement

The factory manager will find it very helpful to have a complete reconciliation of the budgeted profit with the actual profit.

There are two approaches which can be used:

(i) *absorption costing* principles
(ii) *marginal costing* principles

Both methods start with the budgeted profit figure and, using all the variances calculated, reconcile to the actual profit figure. There are only two differences between the methods:

- minor differences in the presentation
- the treatment of the sales volume and fixed overhead volume variances.

8.2   USING ABSORPTION COSTING PRINCIPLES

Using absorption costing principles

This is similar to using the variances shown in Figure 1.1.

Plant Ltd
Reconciliation of the budgeted and actual profit using
absorption costing principles

	£	£	£
Budgeted profit			
12,000 pumps at £26.60 per pump			319,200
Sales variances			
price	25,200 (A)		
volume (profit)	15,960 (F)		
		9,240 (A)	
Cost variances			
Material A			
price	3,000 (A)		
usage	1,320 (F)		
		1,680 (A)	
Material B			
price	15,250 (F)		
usage	10,680 (A)		
		4,570 (F)	
Labour			
rate	6,450 (F)		
idle time	7,200 (A)		
efficiency	13,600 (A)		
		14,350 (A)	
Variable production overhead			
expenditure	8,240 (A)		
efficiency	17,000 (A)		
		25,240 (A)	
Fixed production overhead			
expenditure	12,000 (A)		
volume	18,000 (F)		
		6,000 (F)	
Total net variances			39,940 (A)
Actual profit on 12,600 pumps			**279,260**

8.3   USING MARGINAL COSTING PRINCIPLES

Differences when using marginal costing principles

The layout of the reconciliation statement differs slightly when using marginal costing principles. The key feature of a marginal costing statement is that it highlights the *contribution*.

This has two effects on the reconciliation statement:

(i)   it must highlight the *budgeted contribution* and the *actual contribution*

(ii) all the variances must be presented in terms of their effect on *contribution*.

Highlighting the budgeted contribution and the actual contribution figures involves minor changes to the layout.

Presenting all variances in terms of their effect on contribution effectively involves adding together the fixed production overhead volume variance and the sales volume variance. The reasons are that fixed production overhead costs are *not absorbed* with the marginal costing approach and that the sales volume variance must be expressed in terms of its effect on *contribution* and not in terms of its effect on profit.

Changes in calculations

First, the standard cost card should be represented in marginal costing format (see section 2.2).

Standard marginal costs per unit

		£
Direct material A	1.2 kg × £11 per kg	13.20
Direct material B	4.7 kg × £6 per kg	28.20
Direct labour	90 min × £8 per hour	12.00
Variable production overhead	90 min × £10 per hour	15.00
Total standard marginal cost per unit		**68.40**

Note that fixed production overhead costs are absorbed at a rate per unit only in *absorption costing*.

Second, the actual results for the month must be represented in marginal costing format (see section 2.2).

Actual results for the month in marginal costing format

	£	£
Sales revenue		1,549,800
Variable costs		
Material A	168,000	
Material B	350,750	
Labour	165,550	
Production overhead	214,240	
		898,540
Contribution		651,260
Fixed production overhead		372,000
Actual profit for the month		**279,260**

Third, the sales volume variance must be represented in terms of its effect on *contribution,* not on profit.

Using the standard marginal costing data from section 8.3:

	£
Standard selling price	125.00
Standard marginal cost per unit	68.40
Standard contribution per unit	**56.60**

Note that the standard contribution can also be calculated as:

	£
Standard profit per unit (section 7.3)	26.60
Budgeted fixed production overhead absorption rate per unit	30.00
Standard contribution per unit	**56.60**

Sales volume contribution variance – a definition

The change in contribution caused by sales volume differing from that budgeted.

(budgeted sales × standard contribution per unit) – (actual sales × standard contribution per unit)

		£
S3	Actual sales × standard contribution per unit	
	12,600 × £56.60	713,160
S4	Budgeted sales × standard contribution per unit	
	12,000 × £56.60	679,200
	Sales volume contribution variance	**33,960 (F)**

Using marginal costing principles

This is similar to using the variances shown in Figure 1.2.

Plant Ltd

Reconciliation of the budgeted and actual profit using marginal costing principles

	£	£	£
Budgeted profit			319,200
Add: Budgeted fixed costs			360,000
Budgeted contribution			
12,000 pumps × £56.60 per pump			**679,200**
Sales variances			
price	25,200 (A)		
volume (contribution)	33,960 (F)		
		8,760 (F)	
Cost variances			
Material A			
price	3,000 (A)		
usage	1,320 (F)		
		1,680 (A)	
Material B			
price	15,250 (F)		
usage	10,680 (A)		
		4,570 (F)	
Labour			
rate	6,450 (F)		
idle time	7,200 (A)		
efficiency	13,600 (A)		
		14,350 (A)	
Variable production overhead			
expenditure	8,240 (A)		
efficiency	17,000 (A)		
		25,240 (A)	
Total net variances			27,940 (A)
Actual contribution			**651,260**

	£	£
Actual contribution b/f		651,260
Less: Budgeted fixed production overhead	360,000	
Expenditure variance	12,000 (A)	
i.e. Actual fixed production overhead		372,000
Actual profit on 12,600 pumps		279,260

Notes on the marginal costing presentation

1. The statement follows normal marginal costing and highlights both the *budgeted contribution* and the *actual contribution*.
2. All variances (other than fixed cost variances) are presented in terms of their effect on *contribution*.
3. In order to arrive at the *actual profit*, the *actual fixed costs* must be deducted from the *actual contribution*. However, as this would not normally show the *fixed cost expenditure variance*, the solution is to use the slightly cumbersome method shown.

Budgeted fixed production overhead	360,000	
Expenditure variance	12,000 (A)	
i.e. Actual fixed production overhead		372,000

4. The sales volume contribution variance is £33,960(F). This represents the additional 600 units sold at the standard contribution of £56.60 per pump. As the contribution per pump can be determined as:

	£
Standard profit per unit	26.60
Budgeted fixed production overhead absorption rate per unit	30.00
Standard contribution per unit	56.60

so the sales volume contribution variance of £33,960(F) can be determined as:

	£	
Sales volume profit variance	15,960	(F)
Fixed production overhead volume variance	18,000	(F)
Sales volume contribution variance	33,960	(F)

5. In section 7.4, using absorption costing principles, it was suggested that if it was a deliberate policy to increase the overall profit by reducing the price per pump in order to sell additional pumps, it was not beneficial, as the overall effect on profit was £9,240(A).
This was calculated as:

	£
Sales price variance	25,200 (A)
Sales volume profit variance	15,960 (F)
Total effect on profit	9,240 (A)

If the same information is now presented using marginal costing principles, the effect on profit is very different.

	£
Sales price variance	25,200 (A)
Sales volume contribution variance	33,960 (F)
Total effect on profit	8,760 (F)

This would show that a policy of sales price reduction was beneficial as the reduction was more than compensated for by the additional contribution from the increase in sales volume.

6. The fallacy of the absorption costing statement is that it assumes that additional fixed production overhead costs are absorbed into the cost of production as production is increased.

In the case of Plant Ltd, it assumed that fixed production overhead costs increased by $600 \times £30$, i.e. £18,000, when in practice these costs would be largely constant.

	£
Sales volume variance (profit) using absorption costing	15,960 (F)
Sales volume variance (contribution) using marginal costing	33,960 (F)
Difference accounted for in fixed overhead volume variance by overabsorption of fixed production overhead costs	18,000

Chapter 9

Special considerations

9.1 MATERIAL PURCHASE PRICE VARIANCES

Material price and usage variances

In section 3.1 it was stated that in Plant Ltd, the example used in Chapters 2–8, the material price variance was based on the materials *used*. In practice, materials may be purchased in larger quantities and used over a period of several months. In this case it will be much more useful to calculate the price variance *at the time of purchase* in order to provide immediate feedback to the purchasing manager. All material held in stock will then be valued at the standard cost.

The usage variance will be calculated in the normal way, as and when the materials are issued to production. Note that this is the only way in which the usage variance can be determined in practice, as in order to calculate the usage variance, the actual usage must be compared with the standard usage. The standard usage will not be known until the materials are requisitioned from stores for production.

An example of the material price variance calculated at the time of purchase

Product Zeta requires 8 kg per unit of Material A. Material A has a standard price of £5 per kg. During the month, purchases of Material A were 150,000 kg, costing £825,000. 6,000 units of Zeta were produced and 45,000 kg of Material A were used.

Calculate the material purchase price and usage variances and state the value of the remaining stock of Material A.

Solving the problem

It is not helpful to calculate a direct material total variance, and the format used previously must be adapted.

			£
MV1	*Actual* price of *actual* materials *purchased*		
	£5.50 × 150,000 kg		825,000
MV2	*Standard* price of *actual* materials *purchased*		
	£5 × 150,000 kg		750,000
	Direct material purchase price variance		**75,000 (A)**
MV3	*Standard* price of *actual* materials *used*		
	£5 × 45,000 kg		225,000
MV4	*Standard* price of *standard* materials *used*		
	£5 × 48,000 kg		240,000
	Direct material usage variance		**15,000 (F)**

Remaining stock

	kg
Purchased	150,000
Used in production	45,000
Remaining stock	105,000
Standard price	£5 per kg
Total value	£525,000

9.2 THE COST OF IDLE TIME AND EFFICIENCY VARIANCES

The real cost of labour idle time

In section 4.2 it was stated that if a factory is working at full capacity, any loss of production through idle time is a permanent loss. Quite simply, if production is running seven days each week for 24 hours each day, then it is not possible to recover any production which has been lost, because of a machine breakdown or a shortage of materials, by working additional hours.

The real cost of the labour efficiency variance

In section 5.3 it was stated that an adverse labour efficiency variance can have exactly the same effect as idle time when the factory is working at full capacity, and any loss of production will be a permanent loss.

Conversely, a favourable labour efficiency variance may mean that budgeted production is exceeded and that any additional production will also be sold, generating a substantial benefit in terms of contribution.

Valuing the idle time and efficiency variances

Any loss of production through idle time or labour inefficiency should be valued at its true cost, which is the contribution lost as a direct result of the lost production.

Any increase in production through labour efficiency should be valued in exactly the same way.

9.3   THE COST OF LOST PRODUCTION

An example of lost production

Robbo Ltd has a factory which is working at full capacity to produce hand-held computer games.

The standard data for a game is as follows:

		£
Selling price		40
Materials	0.5 kg × £16 per kg	8
Labour	2 hours × £8 per hour	16
Variable overhead	2 hours × £3 per hour	6
Fixed overhead absorbed		4
Total standard cost		34

Budgeted production for week 41 was 10,000 games.

There was a machine breakdown which resulted in 3,000 idle labour hours.

The actual results for the week were:

Production and sales		8,800 units
		£
Sales revenue		356,400
Materials	4,600 kg	69,000
Labour	20,000 hours paid	160,000
Variable overhead		67,000
Fixed overhead		38,000
Total costs		334,000
Profit		**22,400**

You are required to prepare an analysis of the variances, using marginal costing principles, showing the true cost of the idle time and the labour efficiency and to reconcile the actual profit with the budgeted profit.

Solving the problem

The *standard cost card* has essentially been prepared in the question. The missing information is the standard contribution per unit. The selling price is £40 per unit. The variable standard cost per unit (excluding fixed production overhead) is £30, so the standard contribution per unit is £10.

The *flexible budget* for the *actual* level of production can now be prepared.

Variable standard costs for 8,800 games

		£
Direct material	4,400 kg × £16 per kg	70,400
Direct labour	17,600 hours × £8 per hour	140,800
Variable overhead	17,600 hours × £3 per hour	52,800
Total standard variable cost		**264,000**

Calculating the variances

Materials variances

		£	
M1	Actual price of actual materials used		
	£15 × 4,600 kg	69,000	
M2	Standard price of actual materials used		
	£16 × 4,600 kg	73,600	
	Material price variance	**4,600**	**(F)**

		£	
M2	Standard price of actual materials used		
	£16 × 4,600 kg	73,600	
M3	Standard price of standard materials used		
	£16 × 4,400 kg	70,400	
	Material usage variance	**3,200**	**(A)**

Labour variances

The traditional approach would evaluate the variances as:

		£	
L1	Actual rate for actual hours paid		
	£8 × 20,000 hours	160,000	
L2	Standard rate for actual hours paid		
	£8 × 20,000 hours	160,000	
	Labour rate variance	**0**	

		£	
L2	Standard rate for actual hours paid		
	£8 × 20,000 hours	160,000	
L3	Standard rate for actual hours worked		
	£8 × 17,000 hours	136,000	
	Labour idle time variance	**24,000**	**(A)**

		£	
L3	Standard rate for actual hours worked		
	£8 × 17,000 hours	136,000	
L4	Standard rate for standard hours worked		
	£8 × 17,600 hours	140,800	
	Labour efficiency variance	**4,800**	**(F)**

Disguised in these variances are *two* important factors:

1. The idle time variance represents 3,000 lost hours.
2. There is a labour efficiency variance of 600 hours showing that the actual output was produced in only 17,000 hours, compared with the standard time allowed of 17,600 hours.

Variable production overhead variances

		£	
V1	*Actual* rate for *actual* hours worked		
	17,000 hours	67,000	
V2	*Standard* rate for *actual* hours worked		
	£3 × 17,000 hours	51,000	
	Variable production overhead efficiency		
	variance	**16,000**	**(A)**
V2	*Standard* rate for *actual* hours worked		
	£3 × 17,000 hours	51,000	
V3	*Standard* rate for *standard* hours worked		
	£3 × 17,600 hours	52,800	
	Variable production overhead efficiency		
	variance	**1,800**	**(F)**

Fixed production overhead variance

		£	
F1	*Actual* fixed overhead expenditure	38,000	
F2	*Budgeted* fixed production overhead expenditure		
	10,000 units × £4 per unit	40,000	
	Fixed production overhead expenditure		
	variance	**2,000**	**(F)**

Sales variances

The traditional approach would evaluate the variances as:

		£
S1	*Actual* selling price of *actual* sales volume	
	£40.5 × 8,800 units	356,400
S2	*Standard* selling price of *actual* sales volume	
	£40 × 8,800 units	352,000
	Sales price variance	**4,400** (F)
S3	*Standard* contribution from *actual* sales volume	
	£10 × 8,800	88,000
S4	*Standard* contribution from *budgeted*	
	sales volume	
	£10 × 10,000 units	100,000
	Sales volume contribution variance	**12,000** (A)

Look closely at the sales volume contribution variance. This represents the loss of 1,200 units of sales. The adverse variance would normally be considered to be the responsibility of the sales manager.

It is important to look at the reasons *behind* the variance.

First, there was an idle time variance of 3,000 hours, because of a machine breakdown. 3,000 hours of production time would normally represent 1,500 units of production (at 2 hours per unit).

Second, because of the efficiency of the labour force, an extra 600 standard hours were produced, represented as 300 units (at 2 hours per unit). Remember that a standard hour is a measure of *production* and not of *time*.

The sales volume variance has therefore nothing to do with *sales*, but everything to do with *production*. The loss of 1,200 units should be shown as:

Loss of production due to machine breakdown	1,500 units (A)
Increase in production due to labour efficiency	300 units (F)
Net loss of production	1,200 units (A)

In the statement of variances, these will be valued at the *contribution per unit*, using marginal costing principles.

Reconciliation statement

Robbo Ltd

Reconciliation statement for week 41 using marginal costing principles

	£	£
Budgeted profit:		
10,000 games × £6 profit per unit		60,000
Add: Budgeted fixed costs		40,000
Budgeted contribution		
10,000 games × £10 contribution per unit		100,000
Variances due to machine breakdown		
loss of production		
1,500 units × £10 contribution per unit	15,000 (A)	
labour idle time	24,000 (A)	
		39,000 (A)
Variances due to improved labour efficiency		
increase in production		
300 units × £10 contribution per unit	3,000 (F)	
labour efficiency	4,800 (F)	
variable production overhead efficiency	1,800 (F)	
		9,600 (F)
Other variances		
material price	4,600 (F)	
usage	3,200 (A)	
labour rate	–	
variable production overhead expenditure	16,000 (A)	
sales price	4,400 (F)	
		10,200 (A)
Actual contribution		60,400
Less: Budgeted fixed production overhead	40,000	
Expenditure variance	2,000 (F)	
i.e. Actual fixed production overhead		38,000
Actual profit on 8,800 games		**22,400**

Chapter 10

Materials, labour and sales: mix, yield and quantity variances

10.1 MATERIALS MIX AND YIELD VARIANCES

Materials mix and yield variances

In many process industries, a number of material inputs may be used and the proportions of these can be varied slightly, in order to produce an output of acceptable quantity and quality.

A standard mix is determined, based on a mix that attempts to minimise costs but at the same time meeting quantity and quality requirements. It is possible that a more expensive mix of material may result in a lower process loss, and vice versa. Sometimes a change from the standard mix may be a deliberate decision, based on the prevailing prices of the material ingredients. At other times a shortage of one raw material may force a change in the mix.

By calculating mix and yield variances, it is possible to determine the overall cost of a variation from the standard mix.

The chart of variances from Figure 1.1 may be helpful.

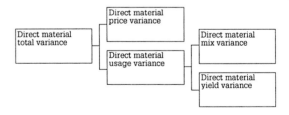

An example of materials mix and yield variances

Westpark Ltd has determined the standard mix for producing 90 litres of Product Z:

	£
50 litres of Material A × £11 per litre	550
30 litres of Material B × £8 per litre	240
20 litres of Material C × £5.50 per litre	110
	900

There is a normal process loss of 10 per cent of the input, which occurs evenly throughout the process.

The actual results for the month were:

	£
52,000 litres of Material A × £10.50 per litre	546,000
28,500 litres of Material B × £8.20 per litre	233,700
19,500 litres of Material C × £5.60 per litre	109,200
	888,900

The output for the month was 91,500 litres.

Calculate the material price, mix and yield variances, reconciling the actual material costs with the standard costs for the actual level of output.

Isolating the variances

Price variances

These can be calculated easily, using the method shown in Chapter 3.

Mix variances

It is easy to see that the standard materials mix has not been used. The actual inputs were not in the budgeted proportions:

Material A	50%
Material B	30%
Material C	20%

The mix variance shows the cost or benefit from deviating from the standard mix.

The actual input was 100,000 litres and the *standard* input proportions would be:

		litres
Material A	50%	50,000
Material B	30%	30,000
Material C	20%	20,000

This can be compared with the *actual* proportions to show the variation in litres:

	standard litres	actual litres	variation
Material A	50,000	52,000	2,000 more
Material B	30,000	28,500	1,500 less
Material C	20,000	19,500	500 less

Note that if the calculations have been done correctly, the net variance (in input quantity) will *always* be zero.

Direct material mix variance – a definition

> Where substitutions within the mix of materials input to a process are possible, the mix variance measures the cost of any variation from the standard mix. The variance, for each input, is based on (i) the change in its weighting within the overall mix, and (ii) whether its unit standard cost is greater or less than the standard weighted average cost of all material inputs. A subdivision of the direct material usage variance.
>
> (actual input quantity – budgeted material input quantity for the output produced) × (standard weighted average cost per input unit – standard cost per input unit)

Yield variance

The yield variance arises when there is a difference between the *actual* output and the *expected* output. Another way of looking at this would be to determine whether the process loss is greater or less than expected.

In the example, there is a normal process loss of 10 per cent, which would be expected to yield 90,000 litres of output from 100,000 litres of input. This month, there is a yield of 91,500 litres, 1,500 litres more than expected. This 1,500 litres represents the yield variance. It is favourable, as the yield is greater than expected.

There is a similarity between the yield variance and the abnormal gain or loss in process costing. See *Process Costing* by the same author in this series.

Direct material yield variance – a definition

Measures the effect on cost of any difference between the actual material usage and that justified by the output produced. It is recommended that this variance is only calculated in total, and not for individual material inputs. A subdivision of the direct material usage variance.

(actual material input quantity – budgeted material input quantity for the output produced) × standard weighted average cost per unit of material input

Calculating the variances

A commonsense approach can be used by those confident in handling variance analysis. For others, an approach is shown which is similar to that used in Chapter 3.

The method follows a logical approach, calculating one variance at a time, but always in the same order:

- price
- mix
- yield.

It may help to use the notes with the solution.

It is especially helpful to calculate the *standard* cost of the *actual* output and the *total* variance at this stage.

Stage 1: Determine the normal cost per litre of output

Standard mix for 90 litres of Product Z	£
50 litres of Material A × £11 per litre	550
30 litres of Material B × £8 per litre	240
20 litres of Material C × £5.50 per litre	110
100	900
10 Normal loss 10%	–
90 Normal cost of output	900

Notes
1. The normal loss has no value, as it has no scrap value.
2. The normal cost per litre of output is calculated as:

$$\frac{\text{Normal cost}}{\text{Output}} = \frac{£900}{90 \text{ litres}} = £10 \text{ per litre}$$

Stage 2: Calculate the total variance

	£
Actual cost of 91,500 litres of output	888,900
Standard cost of 91,500 litres of output	
evaluated at £10 per litre (from Stage 1)	915,000
Total variance	**26,100 (F)**

In Table 10.1, *line 1* presents all the *actual* data. It is essential to have separate columns for *litres* and *£*, and also to have a *total* column. This is used when calculating the *mix* and *yield* variances.

Line 2 represents the *price* variance, which can be determined after calculating line 3. It can be checked as:

		£	
Material A	52,000 litres × £0.50 per litre	26,000	(F)
Material B	28,500 litres × £0.20 per litre	5,700	(A)
Material C	19,500 litres × £0.10 per litre	1,950	(A)
Total net materials variances		**18,350**	**(F)**

Table 10.1: Mix and yield variances

	Material A		Material B		Material C		Total	
	Litres	£	Litres	£	Litres	£	Litres	£
1. Actual price, actual mix, actual quantity	52,000	546,000	28,500	233,700	19,500	109,200	100,000	888,900
2. **Price variance**	–	26,000(F)	–	5,700(A)	–	1,950(A)	–	18,350(F)
3. Standard price, actual mix, actual quantity	52,000	572,000	28,500	228,000	19,500	107,250	100,000	907,250
4. **Mix variance**	2,000	22,000(A)	1,500	12,000(F)	500	2,750(F)	–	7,250(A)
5. Standard price, standard mix, actual quantity	50,000	550,000	30,000	240,000	20,000	110,000	100,000	900,000
6. **Normal loss:** 10% of output							10,000	–
7. Expected output							90,000	900,000
8. **Yield variance**							1,500	15,000(F)
9. Standard price, standard mix, standard quantity							91,500	915,000

Line 3 represents the *standard* price, with the *actual* mix and the *actual* quantity.

Line 4 shows the *mix* variance, which is most easily calculated after entering line 5. Note that a mix variance is *adverse* if *more* than the standard mix has been used and it is *favourable* if *less* than the standard mix has been used. Calculate the physical quantity of the mix variance first. The mix variance is then evaluated at the standard price for each material.

Line 5 represents the *standard* price and the *standard* mix with the *actual* quantity of input. It shows all the input materials at their standard price and standard mix. The total physical quantity of input has not changed from line 1.

Line 6 shows the *normal loss* in processing. In common with process costing the only value ever attributed to a normal loss is its *scrap value* (nil in this case).

Line 7 shows the *expected output.*

Line 8: the *yield* variance must be calculated in conjunction with line 9. The yield variance is always valued at the *normal* cost per unit, as in process costing. In this case it is £10 per litre, as calculated in section 10.4.

Line 9 shows the standard cost of the actual output, again evaluated at the normal cost per unit, £10 per litre.

An alternative method of calculation
The following method of calculation is also shown as an alternative for both sales and labour mix variances. Different methods appeal to different people, so please use the method which is easiest to understand.

	£
Actual price × *actual* mix × *actual* litres	
$(52{,}000 \times £10.50) + (28{,}500 \times £8.20) + (19{,}500 \times £5.60)$	888,900
Standard price × *actual* mix × *actual* litres	
$(52{,}000 \times £11) + (28{,}500 \times £8) + (19{,}500 \times £5.50)$	907,250
Material price variance	**18,350 (F)**

	£
Standard price × *actual* mix × *actual* litres	
$(52{,}000 \times £11) + (28{,}500 \times £8) + (19{,}500 \times £5.50)$	907,250
Standard price × *standard* mix × *actual* litres	
$(50{,}000 \times £11 + (30{,}000 \times £8) + (20{,}000 \times £5.50)$	900,000
Material mix variance	**7,250 (A)**

Standard price × *standard* mix × *actual* litres		
(50,000 × £11) + (30,000 × £8) + (20,000 × £5.50)	900,000	
Standard price × *standard* mix × *standard* litres		
(91,500 × £10)	915,000	
Material yield variance	**15,000**	**(F)**

Summary of variances

Material price variance	18,350	(F)
Material mix variance	7,250	(A)
Material yield variance	15,000	(F)
Total net variances	**26,100**	**(F)**

Another alternative method of calculation

The *mix* variance can also be calculated using the method suggested in the CIMA definition given in section 10.1.

(actual input quantity – budgeted material input quantity for the output produced) ×
(standard weighted average cost per input unit – standard cost per input unit)

Stage 1: Calculate the budgeted material input quantity for the output produced.

The output is 91,500 litres. With a normal loss rate of 10 per cent, the input would need to be:

$$\frac{91,500 \text{ litres}}{0.9} = 101,667 \text{ litres}$$

Stage 2: Actual input quantity – budgeted material input quantity for the output produced

Grade A	52,000 – 50,833 (50% of 101,667 litres)
Grade B	28,500 – 30,500 (30% of 101,667 litres)
Grade C	19,500 – 20,334 (20% of 101,667 litres)

Stage 3: Weighted average cost per input unit

Total costs of 100 litres of input	£900

i.e. weighted average cost per input unit: $\dfrac{£900}{100 \text{ litres}}$ **£9 per litre**

Stage 4: The calculation

	£
Grade A (52,000 – 50,833) × (£11 – £9)	2,334
Grade B (28,500 – 30,500) × (£8 – £9)	2,000
Grade C (19,500 – 20,334) × (£5.50 – £9)	2,916
Material mix variance	7,250 (A)

Although this gives the same net result as the methods used above, the individual material mix variances are different. The method shown here is the preferred CIMA method.

The *yield* variance can also be calculated using the CIMA definition given in above:

(actual material input quantity – budgeted material input quantity for the output produced) × standard weighted average cost per unit of material input

This can be calculated as

Material yield variance

(100,000 litres – 101,667 litres) × £9   **£15,000 (F)**

This gives the same result with all three methods of calculation.

Interpreting the variances

Price variances
There has been a reduction of £0.50 in the standard price of Material A, with small increases in the prices of Material B and Material C. As more than 50 per cent of the input was Material A, this has resulted in a large overall favourable price variance.

Mix variances
There has been a slight change from the standard mix. A higher proportion of Material A has been used, compensated for by slightly lower proportions of Materials B and C. Overall, this is a more costly mix, as a higher proportion of the most expensive material has been used. This is shown by the adverse mix variance of £7,250.

It is possible that the proportions of the mix were varied from the standard mix because of the relative prices of the materials, using more of Material A because it was cheaper this month, and less of Materials B and C. If this is the case, the mix and price variances should be considered together.

	£
Total material price variance	18,350 (F)
Total material mix variance	7,250 (A)
Net overall variance	**11,100 (F)**

This would seem to be a cost-effective decision, as it has resulted in an overall saving of £11,100 (F), as long as there is no adverse effect on the quality or yield.

Yield variance
The yield variance is an additional 1,500 litres, valued at a cost of £10 per litre. This shows that the variation from the standard mix had a beneficial effect on the yield. This is not surprising, as proportionately more of the most expensive Material A was used.

Strategy for the future
Even though the prices of the materials can be expected to change in the future, Westpark Ltd should consider changing the standard mix in order to achieve a higher yield.

The overall effect this month was:

	£
Total material mix variance	7,250 (A)
Material yield variance	15,000 (F)
Net overall variance	**7,750 (F)**

Reconciliation of actual material costs and standard material costs

	£	£
Actual material costs		888,900
Price variances		
A	26,000 (F)	
B	5,700 (A)	
C	1,950 (A)	
		18,350 (F)

Mix variances			
A	22,000 (A)	2,334 (A)	
B	12,000 (F) *or*	2,000 (A)	
C	2,750 (F)	2,916 (A)	
			7,250 (A)
Yield variance			15,000 (F)
Standard cost for the actual level of output			**915,000**

10.2 LABOUR MIX AND YIELD VARIANCES

Labour mix and yield variances

A labour mix variance can arise where different grades of labour, with different rates of pay, are employed together as a team on a particular job. A simple illustration will explain the use of this variance. The standard costs for one unit of Posidon, a new product, are:

skilled workers   10 hours at £12 per hour
unskilled workers   20 hours at £5 per hour

The actual output was 5,600 units and the actual costs were:

		£
skilled workers	54,000 hours costing	648,000
unskilled workers	120,000 hours costing	600,000
	174,000	1,248,000

The principles involved are identical to those used for materials mix and yield variances.

The CIMA chart of variances does not include labour mix and yield variances, but they would be shown as:

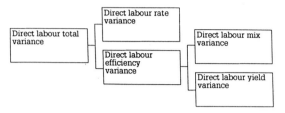

Calculating the variances

The CIMA *Official Terminology* (revised in 1996) does not include labour mix and yield variances.

The same format is used as for materials mix and yield variances. It may help to follow the notes with the solution.

Again, it is helpful to calculate the *standard* cost of the *actual* output and the total variance at this stage.

Stage 1: Determine the standard cost for one unit of output
Standard mix for 1 unit of Posidon:

		£
Skilled workers	10 hours at £12 per hour	120
Unskilled workers	20 hours at £5 per hour	100
		220

Stage 2: Determine the standard cost for 5,600 units of output

		£
Skilled workers	56,000 hours at £12 per hour	672,000
Unskilled workers	112,000 hours at £5 per hour	560,000
Total standard cost of 5,600 units		1,232,000

Stage 3: Calculate the total variance

	£
Actual cost of 5,600 units	1,248,000
Standard cost of 5,600 units evaluated at	
£220 per unit (from Stage 1)	1,232,000
Total variance	**16,000 (A)**

In Table 10.2, *line 1* presents all the *actual* data. It is essential to have separate columns for *hours* and £ and it is helpful to have a *total* column.

Line 2 represents the *rate* variance – nil in this illustration.

Line 3 represents the *standard* rate, with the *actual* mix and the *actual* quantity.

Line 4 shows the *mix* variance, which is most easily calculated after entering line 5. Note that the mix variance is *adverse* if *more* hours than the standard mix have been used and it is *favourable* if *fewer* hours than the standard mix have been used. Calculate the *hours* represented by the mix variance first. The mix variance is then evaluated at the standard rate for each grade of labour.

Line 5 represents the *standard* rate and the *standard* mix for the *actual* hours of input. It shows the inputs at their standard rate and standard mix.

The *total* number of hours has not changed from line 1.

Line 6 shows the *yield* variance which must be calculated in conjunction with line 7.

An alternative way of understanding the yield variance is that 174,000 hours were spent on 5,600 units, which should normally take only 168,000 hours. The extra 6,000 hours is sufficient time to produce an additional 200 units at a normal cost of £220 each i.e. £44,000 in total.

Line 7 shows the standard cost of the actual output.

Table 10.2: Rate, mix and yield variances

		Skilled		Unskilled		Total	
	Hours	£	Hours	£	Hours	£	
1. Actual rate, actual mix, actual quantity	54,000	648,000	120,000	600,000	174,000	1,248,000	
2. Rate variance	—	—	—	—	—	—	
3. Standard rate, actual mix, actual quantity	54,000	648,000	120,000	600,000	174,000	1,248,000	
4. Mix variance	4,000	48,000(F)	4,000	20,000(A)	—	28,000(F)	
5. Standard rate, standard mix, actual quantity	58,000	696,000	116,000	580,000	174,000	1,276,000	
6. Yield variance	2,000	24,000(A)	4,000	20,000(A)	6,000	44,000(A)	
7. Standard rate, standard mix, standard quantity	56,000	672,000	112,000	560,000	168,000	1,232,000	

An alternative method of calculation

	£
Standard rate × *actual* mix × *actual* hours for each grade of labour	
(£12 × 54,000) + (£5 × 120,000)	1,248,000
Standard rate × *standard* mix × *actual* hours	
(£12 × 58,000) + (£5 × 116,000)	1,276,000
Labour mix variance	**28,000 (F)**

	£
Standard rate × *standard* mix × *actual* hours	
(£12 × 58,000) + (£5 × 116,000)	1,276,000
Standard rate × *standard* mix × *standard* hours	
(£12 × 56,000) + (£5 × 112,000)	1,232,000
Labour yield variance	**44,000 (A)**

Summary of variances

	£
Labour mix variance	28,000 (F)
Labour yield variance	44,000 (A)
Labour efficiency variance	**16,000 (A)**

Interpreting the variances

Rate variances
These are interpreted as for normal labour rate variances (see Chapter 4).

Mix variances
There has been a change from the standard mix. A higher proportion of unskilled labour has been used, compensated for by a lower proportion of skilled labour. This is shown by the favourable mix variance of £28,000. It is possible that this has arisen because of a shortage of skilled labour.

Yield variance
The yield variance shows that there was an adverse yield of 6,000 hours, comparing the actual hours of input with the standard hours of output. This would normally be sufficient to produce an additional 200 units.

It is possible that the adverse yield variance arose because of the favourable mix variance. As proportionately more of the unskilled labour was used, this could affect the level of output.

In this case, it would be advisable to consider the net effect of the mix and yield variances.

	£	
Total labour mix variance	28,000	(F)
Total labour yield variance	44,000	(A)
Net overall variance	**16,000**	**(A)**

It would not be advisable to repeat the alteration to the mix variance in the future as it has a substantial adverse effect on the yield.

Note that as there is no labour rate variance; the total variance is equivalent to the normal labour efficiency variance.

10.3 SALES MIX AND QUANTITY VARIANCES

Sales mix and quantity variances

If a firm sells a variety of different products, each with a different profit margin, the sales volume variance can be analysed into a sales mix variance and a sales quantity variance. These can be calculated either on the basis of the *profit* per unit, using absorption costing principles, or on the basis of the *contribution* per unit, using marginal costing principles.

The calculation of the sales mix variance is especially appropriate where the products are to some degree interchangeable, for example different models of the same product.

The chart of variances in Figure 1.1 may be helpful.

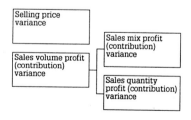

Sales mix profit (contribution) variance – a definition

> The change in profit (contribution) caused by a change in the mix of products or services sold.
>
> (actual sales units × budgeted weighted average standard profit (contribution) per unit) – (actual sales units × individual standard profit (contribution) per unit)
>
> This method of computation highlights the profit (contribution) effect, by product, of selling products whose individual standard profits (contributions) differ from the budgeted weighted average standard profit (contribution)

The calculation of the sales quantity variance is the 'other' part of the sales volume variance not accounted for by the mix variance.

Sales quantity profit (contribution) variance – a definition

> The change in profit (contribution) caused by a difference between actual and budgeted sales quantities. It is assumed that the actual sales mix is in budgeted proportions.
>
> (budgeted sales units × budgeted weighted average standard profit (contribution) per unit) – (total actual sales units × budgeted weighted average standard profit (contribution) per unit

A simple illustration

Fastgrow Ltd produces three different grades of fertiliser in 5 kilo bags. The budgeted sales for week 24 were:

	Bags	Standard contribution per bag £	Total contribution £
Grade A	4,000	8	32,000
Grade B	3,500	6	21,000
Grade C	2,500	3	7,500
	10,000		60,500

The actual sales for week 24 were:

	Bags	Standard contribution per bag £	Total contribution £
Grade A	3,000	8	24,000
Grade B	4,000	6	24,000
Grade C	4,000	3	12,000
	11,000		60,000
Total sales volume variance			500 (A)

This assumes that there is no sales price variance and that costs are as standard. If the costs were not as standard, these would be shown as *cost variances* and would not affect the analysis of *sales variances*.

A sales volume variance would show that an additional 1,000 bags were sold, but that the contribution fell by £500 overall. It is much easier to understand why this occurred if a *sales mix variance* is calculated.

Calculating the variances

The same format can be used as for materials mix and yield variances. See Table 10.3 for the solution. It may help to follow the notes with the solution.

In Table 10.3, *line 1* represents all the *actual* data. The £ column should represent the total *profit* or *contribution*, not the total revenue, as all variances are calculated in terms of their effect on profit or contribution.

Line 2 represents the *sales price* variance – nil in this illustration.

Line 3 represents the *standard* price, with the *actual* mix and the *actual* quantity.

Line 4 shows the *mix* variance, which is most easily calculated after entering line 5. Note that the mix variance is *favourable* if *more* units than the standard mix have been sold and is *adverse* if *fewer* units than the standard mix have been sold. This is the opposite of the cost variances. Calculate the bags represented by the standard mix (line 5) first, then determine the *number of bags* represented by the mix variance, and finally evaluate this at the standard contribution (or profit per unit).

Line 5 represents the *standard* price and the *standard* mix for the *actual* bags sold. The total number of bags has not changed from line 1.

Table 10.3: Price, mix and quantity variance

	Grade A		Grade B		Grade C		Total	
	Bags	Total cont'n	Bags	Total cont'n	Bags	Total cont'n	Bags	Total cont'n
1. Actual price, actual mix, actual quantity	3,000	24,000	4,000	24,000	4,000	12,000	11,000	60,000
2. **Price variance**	—	—	—	—	—	—	—	—
3. Standard price, actual mix, actual quantity	3,000	24,000	4,000	24,000	4,000	12,000	11,000	60,000
4. **Mix variance**	1,400	11,200(A)	150	900(F)	1,250	3,750(F)	—	6,550(A)
5. Standard price, standard mix, actual quantity	4,400	35,200	3,850	23,100	2,750	8,250	11,000	66,550
6. **Quantity variance**	400	3,200(F)	350	2,100(F)	250	750(F)	1,000	6,050(F)
7. Standard price, standard mix, standard quantity, i.e. budgeted sales	4,000	32,000	3,500	21,000	2,500	7,500	10,000	60,500

Line 6 shows the *sales quantity* variance which compares the actual and budgeted sales volumes, assuming both are in the standard mix. Some texts further analyse the sales quantity variance into market size and market share variances.

Line 7 shows the *standard* price, *standard* mix and *standard* quantity, i.e. the budgeted level of sales, evaluated at the standard contribution per unit.

An alternative method of calculation

The sales mix and sales quantity variances can also be calculated in the following manner:

	£	
Actual mix × *actual* bags at *standard* contribution per bag		
$(3,000 \times £8) + (4,000 \times £6) + (4,000 \times £3)$	60,000	
Standard mix × *actual* bags at *standard* contribution per bag		
$(4,400 \times £8) + (3,850 \times £6) + (2,750 \times £3)$	66,550	
Sales mix variance	**6,550**	**(A)**
Standard mix × *actual* bags at *standard* contribution per bag		
$(4,400 \times £8) + (3,850 \times £6) + (2,750 \times £3)$	66,550	
Standard mix × *standard* bags at *standard* contribution per bag		
$(4,000 \times £8) + (3,500 \times £6) + (2,500 \times £3)$	60,500	
Sales quantity variance	**6,050**	**(F)**

Summary of variances

Sales mix variance	6,550	(A)
Sales quantity variance	6,050	(F)
Sales volume variance	**500**	**(A)**

Another alternative method of calculation

The *mix* variance can also be calculated using the CIMA definition given on page 73.

(actual sales units × budgeted weighted average standard profit

(contribution) per unit) – (actual sales units × individual standard profit

(contribution) per unit)

Stage 1: Actual sales units × budgeted weighted average standard contribution per unit

11,000 units × £6.05   **£66,550**

Budgeted weighted average standard contribution per unit is calculated as:

$$\frac{\text{Budgeted total contribution}}{\text{Budgeted units}} = \frac{£60,500}{10,000 \text{ units}} = \textbf{£6.05}$$

Stage 2: Actual sales units × individual standard contribution per unit

		£
Grade A	3,000 × £8	24,000
Grade B	4,000 × £6	24,000
Grade C	4,000 × £3	12,000
		60,000

Sales mix variance

£66,550 – £60,000   **£6,550 (A)**

The *quantity* variance can also be calculated using the CIMA definition given on page 73.

(budgeted sales units × budgeted weighted average standard profit (contribution)

per unit) – (total actual sales units × budgeted weighted average standard profit

(contribution) per unit)

Stage 1: Budgeted sales units × budgeted weighted average standard contribution per unit

10,000 units × £6.05   **£60,500**

Stage 2: Total actual sales units × budgeted weighted average standard contribution per unit

    11,000 units × £6.05   **£66,550**

Sales quantity variance
    £60,500 − £66,550   **£6,050 (F)**

Interpreting the variances

Price variances
These are interpreted as for normal sales price variances (see Chapter 7).

Mix variances
There has been a change from the standard mix. A higher proportion of the less profitable Grades B and C has been sold, compensated for by a lower proportion of the more profitable Grade A. This is shown by the adverse mix variance of £6,550.

Quantity variances
These show the effect of a change in the relative mix of the grades sold. If the originally budgeted sales mix had been maintained, then the contribution would have increased by £6,050 for the actual level of sales. This compares with the present adverse sales volume variance of £500.

Chapter 11

Planning and operational variances

11.1 CAUSES OF VARIANCES

Explanation

Many accountants believe that the information provided by traditional variance analysis is failing to provide them with the information they require for control purposes. Much of the criticism stems from the fact that if circumstances have changed, the original standards will no longer be valid. Any reports showing variations from standards should show the effect of two different aspects:

- the degree to which a 'reasonable' or 'currently' attainable standard may have changed; and
- the degree to which the actual results might conform with an up to date standard.

Causes of variances

Bromwich identified *five* major causes of variances as:

(i)   inefficiency in operation, i.e. a failure to achieve a reasonable standard through inability or lack of motivation;
(ii) incorrect plans or standards, or originally correct plans and standards which have been invalidated by environment changes. In this case, the reporting of variances may lead to the revision of plans. This is clearly a situation where managers should not be encouraged to try to keep to the original plans;
(iii) poor communication of standards and budgetary goals;
(iv) random fluctuations around standards and budgetary goals (which are likely to be average targets);
(v)   if in budgeting (and in decision-making) the interdependence of departments has not been taken into account, then action taken by one department may cause variances elsewhere in the firm.

Bromwich stated that variance analysis designed with these different causes in mind will be much more useful to management than the 'ritual calculation' of all-purpose textbook variances.

For cause (iii) *poor communication*, the theoretical background is still lacking. For cause iv) *random fluctuations*, statistical methods have been developed. For cause (v) *interdependence* between departments, the theory is being developed through the use of transfer prices.

The variances attributable to cause (i) *inefficiency and poor motivation* are known as *operational variances*. The variances highlighting cause (ii) *invalid plans and standards* are known as *planning variances*.

General approach

The most simple approach to solving such variance problems is to revise the original budget to take account of the information now available. This introduces an additional intermediate step in the determination of the variances, which enables the planning and operational variances to be calculated easily.

Traditional approach	Operational and planning approach
Original budget	Original (ex ante) budget
	Planning variances
Traditional variances	Revised (ex post) budget
	Operational variances
Actual results	Actual results

The traditional approach compares the original budget with the actual results to arrive at the total variance.

The operational and planning approach goes one step further and analyses the total variance into a *planning variance*, which shows the variance due to changes in the environment, and an *operational variance*, which shows the result of a change in the level of efficiency.

11.2 PLANNING AND OPERATIONAL VARIANCES

The planning variance

The planning variance shows the difference between the original (ex ante) budget and the revised (ex post) budget. It is an attempt to evaluate the planning department. If there is *any* planning variance at all, this simply shows that the planning department was wrong in its original predictions. The best planning variance is zero.

A planning variance will also be labelled as favourable or adverse. This does not refer to whether the planning department has achieved its target, but much like any other variance, it simply shows how the revised budget compares with the original budget.

If the effect of the revised budget is to increase the original budgeted profit because of a favourable change in circumstances for the firm, then the planning variance is favourable. If, however, the effect of the revised budget is to reduce the original budgeted profit because of an unfavourable change in circumstances for the firm, then the planning variance is adverse.

The operational variance

The operational variance shows the difference between the revised (ex post) budget and the actual results. It is an attempt to evaluate how efficiently the operations have been carried out *in the prevailing circumstances.*

An operational variance will be favourable if it increases the profits of the firm and adverse if it reduces the profits. The calculation of the variance and the allocation of responsibility is similar to that of the traditional variances.

11.3 AN ILLUSTRATION

A year ago Kenp Ltd entered the market for the manufacture and sale of a revolutionary insulating material. The budgeted production and sales volumes were 1000 units. The originally estimated sales price and standard costs for this new product were as follows.

	£	£
Standard sales price (per unit)		100
Standard costs (per unit)		
Raw materials (Aye 10 kg at £5 per kg)	50	
Labour (6 hours at £4 per hour)	24	
		74
Standard contribution (per unit)		26

Actual first-year results were:

	£	£
Sales (1000 units)		158,000
Production costs (100 units)		
Raw materials (Aye 10,800 kg)	97,200	
Labour (5,800 hours)	34,800	
		132,000
Actual contribution		26,000

'Throughout the year we attempted to operate as efficiently as possible, given the prevailing conditions,' stated the managing director. 'Although in total the performance agreed with budget, in every detailed respect, except volume, there were large differences. These were due, mainly, to the tremendous success of the new insulating material which created increased demand both for the product itself and all the manufacturing resources used in its production. This then resulted in price rises all round.

'Sales were made at what was felt to be the highest feasible price but, it was later discovered, our competitors sold for £165 per unit and we could have equalled this price. Labour costs rose dramatically with increased demand for the specialist skills required to produce the product and the general market rate was £6.25 per hour – although Kenp always paid below the general market rate whenever possible.

'Raw material Aye was chosen as it appeared cheaper than the alternative material Bee which could have been used. The costs which were expected at the time the budget was prepared were (per kg): Aye, £5 and Bee, £6. However, the market prices relating to efficient purchases of the materials during the year were:

- Aye £8.50 per kg; and
- Bee £7.00 per kg.

'Therefore it would have been more appropriate to use Bee, but as production plans were based on Aye it was Aye that was used.

'It is not proposed to request a variance analysis for the first year's results as most of the deviations from budget were caused by the new product's great success and this could not have been fully anticipated and planned for. In any event the final contribution was equal to that originally budgeted so operations must have been fully efficient.'

Required
(a) Compute the traditional variances for the first year's operations.
(b) Prepare an analysis of variances for the first year's operations which will be useful in the circumstances of Kenp Ltd. The analysis should indicate the extent to which the variances were due to operational efficiency or planning causes.
(c) Using, for illustration, a comparison of the raw material variances computed in (a) and (b) above, briefly outline two major advantages and two major disadvantages of the approach applied in part (b) over the traditional approach.

Solving the problem
(a) *Traditional variances*

	£
Sales price variance	
(£158 – £100) × 1,000 units	58,000 (F)
Sales volume variance	0
Material price variance	
(£9 – £5) × 10,800 kg	43,200 (A)
Material usage variance	
(10,800 kg – 10,000 kg) × £5	4,000 (A)
Labour rate variance	
(£6 – £4) × 5,800 hours	11,600 (A)
Labour efficiency variance	
(5,800 – 6,000 hours) × £4	800 (F)
Total net variances	0

(b) *Useful analysis of the variances in the first year of operation*

In each case the variance should be shown as being attributable to planning or to operational reasons. Many of the original standards which were set became outdated during the year because of changes in prices and wage rates. In addition, Kenp Ltd has made the wrong decision concerning its choice of material. This also makes the calculations slightly more complex, so the material variances will be dealt with after the sales and labour variances.

STEP 1 – REVISED (EX POST) BUDGET

The objective with all the variance calculations is to set up a revised budget which evaluates both the planning and operational efficiency of the managers. This is based on what the firm might reasonably expect to have achieved in the circumstances, with the benefit of hindsight.

The original budget is inaccurate in terms of both the selling price per unit and the labour rate per hour. Competitors sold their products for £165 per unit and Kenp could have equalled that price. Labour costs rose dramatically and the general market rate was £6.25 per hour.

Although the actual results are based on the use of material Aye, which was chosen because it was expected to be cheaper, in practice material Bee was cheaper and the variances should highlight the cost of making the wrong decision.

STEP 2 – SALES VARIANCES

		Quantity	Price per unit	Total
			£	£
S1	Original (ex ante) budget	1,000	100	100,000
	Planning variances			
S2	Revised (ex post) budget	1,000	165	165,000
	Operational variances			
S3	Actual results	1,000	158	158,000

The *planning* variances are calculated by comparing lines S1 and S2. The calculations are identical to those for traditional variance analysis and this can result in both a price and a volume variance (which would be evaluated at the revised standard profit or contribution per unit).

The *planning price* variance is

(£165 − £100) × 1,000 units   65,000 (F)

It is favourable as the increase in price has a beneficial effect on the firm's original budgeted profit.

The *operational* variances are calculated by comparing lines S2 and S3. Again the calculations are identical to those for traditional variance analysis and it can result in both a price and a volume variance.

The *operational price* variance is

(£165 − £158) × 1,000 units   7,000 (A)

It is adverse as the firm did not take advantage of the opportunity to sell the product for £165 per unit, losing £7,000 profit in the process.

STEP 3 − LABOUR VARIANCES

		Hours	Rate per hour	Total
			£	£
L1	Original (ex ante) budget	6,000	4.00	24,000
	Planning variances			
L2	Revised (ex post) budget	6,000	6.25	37,500
	Operational variances			
L3	Actual results	5,800	6.00	34,800

The *planning* variances are calculated by comparing lines L1 and L2. Again the calculations are identical to those for traditional variance analysis and this can result in both a rate and an efficiency variance.

The *planning rate* variance is

(£6.25 − £4.00) × 6,000 hours   13,500 (A)

It is adverse as the general increase in labour rates has a detrimental effect on the budgeted profit.

The *operational* variances are calculated by comparing lines L2 and L3. This can result in both a rate and an efficiency variance.

The *operational rate* variance is

(£6.00 − £6.25) × 5,800 hour   1,450 (F)

It is favourable as the firm paid less than the general market rate of £6.25 per hour.

The *operational efficiency* variance is

$(5,800 - 6,000) \times £6.25$ 1,250 (F)

It is favourable as the labour force took less time than expected.

STEP 4 – MATERIAL VARIANCES

The analysis of the material variances is more complex as there are two planning errors (and variances) as well as the usual operational variances. One planning error was the inability to predict accurately the price of material Aye. The other planning error relates to the fact that material Bee was cheaper than material Aye, although the reverse situation was predicted.

In this example, it is necessary to prepare *two* ex post budgets, one for material Aye and one for material Bee.

		Kg	Price per kg £	Total £
M1	Original (ex ante) budget – Aye	10,000	5.00	50,000
	Planning variances			
M2	Revised (ex post) budget – Bee	10,000	7.00	70,000
	Planning variances			
M3	Revised (ex post) budget – Aye	10,000	8.50	85,000
	Operational variances			
M4	Actual results – Aye	10,800	9.00	97,200

The first *planning* variance is an attempt to show that there has been a general increase in the price of raw materials.

This *planning price* variance is

$(£7 - £5) \times 10,000$ kg   20,000 (A)

It is adverse as a general increase in prices will cause a reduction from the budgeted profit. It is considered to be *uncontrollable* or *unavoidable* as, whichever material was chosen, it would be impossible to avoid paying less than £7 per kg.

The second *planning* variance is an attempt to show the cost of choosing the wrong material, in terms of price. Material Bee was generally available at £7 per kg, £1.50 per kg less than the price of material Aye at £8.50 per kg.

This *planning price* variance is:

(£8.50 – £7.00) × 10,000 kg   15,000 (A)

It shows the cost of choosing the wrong material input. It is normally classified as possibly avoidable as the purchasing manager should have been able to predict the relative movement in prices with greater accuracy.

When considering the cost of choosing the wrong material, it is important that lines M2 and M3 are in the correct order. M1 will always be the originally budgeted material and M4 will always be the actual results. One way to ensure the correct order is to remember that, in order to calculate an operational variance, both M3 and M4 must be based on the material actually used – material Aye in this example. The only place left for the ex post budget for material Bee is then in line M2.

The *operational variances* are calculated by comparing lines M3 and M4. In this example, it will result in both a price and a usage variance.

The *operational price* variance is

(£9 – £8.50) × 10,000 kg   5,000 (A)

It is adverse as the price paid was greater than the market price for efficient purchases.

The *operational usage* variance is

(10,800 – 10,000) × £8.50   6,800 (A)

It is adverse as the actual usage was greater than the standard usage.

The operational variances are considered to be controllable or avoidable and in this example are both attributable to operational inefficiencies.

(c) *The traditional approach compared with the planning and operational approach*

ADVANTAGES OF THE PLANNING AND OPERATIONAL APPROACH

The material price variance can be analysed into the different elements which are avoidable, possibly avoidable and unavoidable. This provides very useful information for evaluating the performance of the purchasing manager and more information for evaluating the effectiveness of the price standards.

The material usage variance is evaluated in a more meaningful manner, as the real cost to the firm of the excess usage is nearer to £8.50 per kg (as in the operational variance) than the original standard of £5 per kg (as in the traditional variance).

DISADVANTAGES OF THE PLANNING AND OPERATIONAL APPROACH
It is difficult to classify the variances as avoidable, possibly avoidable and unavoidable, and to some extent it is subjective.

The determination of the ex post standards, which are incorporated into the revised budget, may also be subjective. The estimates must be obtained from the best data available. This may be one person's opinion of what is reasonable. However, even these estimates will usually be more useful than outdated standards.

11.4 LIMITATIONS AND JUSTIFICATION

Limitations of planning and operational variances

Setting an ex post budget inevitably involves some judgement. It is often difficult, even with hindsight, to decide what a realistic standard should have been. It would be easy to justify all variances as planning variances so that there are no operational variances.

Where different materials are used as substitutes for each other, the planning variances assume that these materials are perfect substitutes. In practice this may not be so.

Justification for using planning and operational variances

Variances, especially price variances, can be analysed into those elements which are controllable, possibly avoidable and uncontrollable. This provides management with more information for evaluating the performance of the departmental managers. Although the information may not be perfect, it is more helpful than no information.

The variances can be evaluated in a more meaningful manner. For example, the material usage variance is evaluated at £5 per kg using the traditional approach, but at £8.50 per kg using the planning and operational approach. This method is more likely to reflect the 'real' cost or saving resulting from a usage variance.

Chapter 12

The effect of the learning curve on variance analysis

12.1 THE LEARNING CURVE

Learning curves and standard-setting

During the Second World War, aircraft manufacturers discovered that labour unit cost declined as a function of the cumulative number of units produced, and that the decline in unit cost could be predicted accurately. This is known as the learning phenomenon and can be shown graphically as a learning curve.

The effects of learning

When new products or processes are introduced, learning occurs and productivity increases. The learning curve is particularly applicable to the early phases of a complex and labour-intensive operation.

12.2 DIFFERENT METHODS OF CALCULATION

An example of the learning phenomenon

The patterns developed in learning curves show the percentage reduction in the average direct labour input time per unit required as the cumulative output doubles.

The following example illustrates a learning curve of 80 per cent.

Batch size	Cumulative number	Total time taken hours	Average time per unit hours
1	1	100	100
1	2	160	80
2	4	256	64
4	8	409.6	51.2
8	16	655.36	40.96
16	32	1,048.576	32.768

Note that the average time per unit is 80 per cent of the previous average time per unit.

The graphical method of presentation

The graph in Figure 12.1 is plotted from the cumulative number of units and the average time per unit shown above.

Figure 12.1: The learning curve

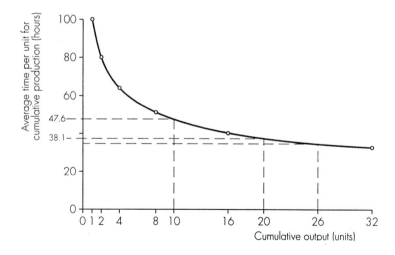

This shows that the average time per unit declines rapidly in the early stages and then more slowly in the later stages. When normal efficiency is achieved, this is known as the steady-state production level.

In order to determine the total hours required, the average hours per unit must be multiplied by the cumulative units produced.

The graphical method is more useful than the tabular method as it is possible to interpolate and determine the average time for 12 units, 20 units or any other number required.

The mathematical approach

The learning curve can be expressed in equation form:

$$Y_x = aX^b$$

where:

Y_x = the cumulative average time to produce Y units.

a = the time required to produce the first unit of output.

x = the number of units under consideration.

The exponent, b, is the logarithm of the learning curve improvement rate divided by the logarithm of 2.

For example, for an 80 per cent learning curve, using natural logarithms:

$$b = \frac{\log 0.8}{\log 0.2} = \frac{-0.2231}{0.6931} = -0.322$$

The *cumulative* average time taken to produce 10 units if the first unit took 100 hours can be calculated as:

$$Y_{10} = 100 \times 10^{-0.322}$$
$$= 100 \times 0.476$$
$$= 47.6 \text{ hours}$$

The cumulative average time taken to produce 10 units if the first unit took 100 hours would be:

$$Y_{20} = 100 \times 20^{-0.322}$$
$$= 100 \times 0.381$$
$$= 38.1 \text{ hours}$$

12.3 INCREMENTAL COSTS

Learning curves and incremental costs

In many situations, the most useful application for the learning curve will be in terms of its incremental cost. This is not provided by the formula, but it can be obtained easily.

Refer to the example in section 12.2 and Figure 12.1.

Assume that the firm has already produced 16 units and wishes to calculate the cost of an additional 10 units, assuming a labour rate of £12 per hour.

Cumulative output of 26 units will take an average time of:

$$Y_{26} = 100 \times 26^{-0.322}$$
$$= 100 \times 0.350$$
$$= 35 \text{ hours}$$

or reading from the graph, 35 hours.

The first 16 units took an average of 40.96 hours each (from the data in section 12.2), i.e. a total of 655.36 hours.

The cumulative output of 26 units took an average of 35 hours each, i.e. a total of 910 hours.

The additional 10 units will therefore take:

Total time for 26 units	910.00 hours
Total time for 16 units	655.36 hours
Time for additional 10 units	254.64 hours

The firm will then be able to determine the labour cost for the additional 10 units – 254.64 hours at £12 per hour, i.e. £3055.68.

Learning curves and costs

The application of the learning curve helps to predict the cumulative average labour time required per unit.

This can then be used to determine the total labour hours required and subsequently the additional labour hours required for a certain number of units. This means that a reasonably accurate prediction of labour costs can be made. It can also be used to predict *variable production overhead costs*, where these vary in direct proportion to labour hours worked.

It does *not* apply to material costs, non-variable costs or costs that vary in proportion to output rather than input.

12.4 LEARNING CURVE APPLICATIONS

Applications of the learning curve

Learning curve applications are most important where there is substantial labour input and the activity is complex. In practice, the rate of learning may vary between 70 per cent and 90 per cent. A major drawback is that the actual rate of learning will never be known at the start of a new process. However, in a complex situation with a large labour input, it is better to have some estimate than none.

Pricing decisions

Learning curves enable costs to be predicted with greater accuracy. In turn, this should lead to a better pricing decision. This could be particularly helpful where the firm has been operating the process for a short time and so already has a reduced level of costs. Alternatively, merely being able to recognise that learning takes place could give a firm a substantial advantage over its competitors when quoting a price to supply a new component.

Work scheduling

An understanding of learning curves can increase the firm's ability to predict labour requirements. Production and delivery schedules can be determined with greater accuracy. This should enable better maintenance scheduling, quality control, material purchasing and sales promotion to be carried out. This should result in improved customer relations.

Standard-setting and motivation

If the learning phenomenon is taken into account when setting standards, both the standards and the resulting variances will be more meaningful. If standards are set without regard to the learning curve, this may result in standards which can be achieved too easily and will lead to loss of motivation. If standards are set during the learning period, based on steady-state conditions, this will also lead to loss of motivation as the standards will be considered unattainable.

Overtime decisions

If a firm is near the start of its learning curve and has a production target to meet in a limited period of time, it would be more advisable to authorise overtime working than to employ additional workers, who would not be needed subsequently.

12.5 LEARNING CURVES APPLIED TO VARIANCE ANALYSIS

An example of learning curves applied to variance analysis

Boats Ltd has developed a new type of speedboat called the T9 which is expected to be sold in small quantities. Construction of the T9 in Boats Ltd's yard is a continuous assembly operation in which the majority of costs are labour-related. Assembly of the T9 involves the services of two separate classes of labour – skilled (at a standard rate of £12.50 per hour) and semi-skilled (at a standard rate of £9.50 per hour).

Experience on producing other models in Boats Ltd's yard has shown that the use of skilled labour is associated with an 80 per cent learning curve effect, and the use of semi-skilled labour is associated with a 90 per cent learning curve effect.

Labour usage for the first T9 assembled was as follows, being adopted as the initial standard:

Skilled	476 hours
Semi-skilled	325 hours

In June, the sixth and seventh T9s were assembled from start to finish. During June the following labour usage and costs were recorded:

Skilled	340 hours	(cost £4,002)
Semi-skilled	628 hours	(cost £6,406)

After inspecting the cost variance analysis for June, Boats Ltd's finance director gives the following instruction:

'I would be interested to see how far the labour efficiency variance is caused by a departure from the standard mix of skilled and semi-skilled labour (let us call this the labour mix variance) and how far it is caused by the overall output achieved by the workforce (let us call this the labour output variance).'

Required

(a) Calculate the standard labour costs of the T9s assembled in June; reconcile this standard with actual costs by calculating rate and efficiency variances.

(b) Split the labour efficiency variance into 'labour mix' and 'labour output' variances as required by Boats Ltd's finance director.

(c) Write a memorandum to the finance director explaining why you consider the exercise he has specified (see requirement (b)) is or is not worthwhile.

Note: learning curve effects may be appraised using the cumulative average time model and the formula $y = a/x_n$, where y is the cumulative average hours per unit, a is hours for the first unit, x is the number of units produced and n is 0.322 (80 per cent curve) or 0.152 (90 per cent curve).

Solving the problem

(a) *Standard costs, rate and efficiency variances*

In order to calculate the time taken to assemble the sixth and seventh T9s in June, it is necessary to determine the total cumulative time taken to assemble the first five T9s.

Skilled Labour

$$y = 476 \times x^{-0.322}$$

After five T9s:

$$y = 476 \times 5^{-0.322}$$
$$= 283.5 \text{ hours per boat}$$

The total cumulative time taken to assemble the first five T9s will be:

$$283.5 \times 5 = 1417.5 \text{ hours}$$

After seven T9s:

$$y = 476 \times 7^{-0.322}$$
$$= 254.4 \text{ hours per boat}$$

The total cumulative time taken to assemble the first seven T9s will be:

$$254.4 \times 7 = 1,780.8 \text{ hours}$$

The standard time for boats six and seven will be:

$$1780.8 - 1417.5 = 363.3 \text{ hours}$$

The standard cost will be:

$$363.3 \times £12.5 \text{ per hour} = £4541.25$$

SEMI-SKILLED LABOUR

$$y = 325 \times x^{-0.152}$$

After five T9s:

$$y = 325 \times 5^{-0.152}$$
$$= 254.5 \text{ hours per boat}$$

The total cumulative time taken to assemble the first five T9s will be:

$$254.5 \times 5 = 1272.5 \text{ hours}$$

After seven T9s:

$$y = 325 \times 7^{-0.152}$$
$$= 241.8 \text{ hours per boat}$$

The total cumulative time taken to assemble the first seven T9s will be:

$$241.8 \times 7 = 1692.6 \text{ hours}$$

The standard time for boats six and seven will be:

$$1692.6 - 1272.5 \text{ hours} = 420.1 \text{ hours}$$

The standard cost will be:

$$420.1 \text{ hours} \times £9.50 \text{ per hour} = £3990.95$$

LABOUR RATE VARIANCES

	£
Skilled labour	
Actual rate for *actual* hours worked	
340 hours	4,002
Standard rate for *actual* hours worked	
£12.50 × 340 hours	4,250
Skilled labour rate variance	**248 (F)**

Semi-skilled labour	£
Actual rate for *actual* hours worked	
628 hours	6,406
Standard rate for *actual* hours worked	
£9.50 × 628 hours	5,966
Semi-skilled labour rate variance	**440 (A)**

LABOUR EFFICIENCY VARIANCES

Skilled labour	£
Standard rate for *actual* hours worked	
£12.50 × 340 hours	4,250
Standard rate for *standard* hours allowed	
£12.50 × 363.3 hours	4,541.25
Skilled labour efficiency variance	**291.25 (F)**

Semi-skilled labour	£
Standard rate for *actual* hours worked	
£9.50 × 628 hours	5,966
Standard rate for *standard* hours allowed	
£9.50 × 420.1 hours	3,990.95
Semi-skilled labour efficiency variance	**1,975.05 (A)**

Reconciliation

	Skilled labour	*Semi-skilled labour*
	£	£
Standard labour costs	4,541.25	3,990.95
Rate variances	248.00 (F)	440.00 (A)
Efficiency variances	291.25 (F)	1,975.05 (A)
Actual labour costs	4,002.00	6,406.00

(b) *Labour mix and labour output variances*

	Skilled labour hours	Skilled labour £	Semi-skilled labour hours	Semi-skilled labour £	Total hours	Total £
1. Standard rate actual mix actual hours	340	4,250	628	5,966	968	10,216
2. Mix variance	109	1,362.5(F)	109	1,035.5(A)	–	327(F)
3. Standard rate standard mix actual hours	449	5,612.5	519	4,930.5	968	10,543
4. Output/yield variance	85.7	1,071.25(A)	98.9	939.55(A)	184.6	2,010.8(A)
5. Standard rate standard mix standard hours	363.3	4,541.25	420.1	3,990.95	783.4	8,532.2

NOTES

1. The standard mix is calculated from

Skilled labour – standard hours	363.3	46.4%
Semi-skilled labour – standard hours	420.1	53.6%
	783.4	

2. When applied to the actual hours, the standard mix is

Skilled labour	968 × 46.4%	449
Semi-skilled labour	968 × 53.6%	519
Total hours		968

AN ALTERNATIVE METHOD OF CALCULATION

	£
Standard rate × *actual* mix × *actual* hours for each grade of labour (£12.50 × 340) + (£9.50 × 628)	10,216
Standard rate × *standard* mix × *actual* hours for each grade of labour (£12.50 × 449) + (£9.50 × 519)	10,543
Mix variance	**327 (F)**

	£
Standard rate × *standard* mix × *actual* hours for each grade of labour	
(£12.50 × 449) + (£9.50 × 519)	10,543
Standard rate × *standard* mix × *standard* hours for each grade of labour	
(£12.50 × 363.3) + (£9.50 × 420.1)	8,532.2
Output (yield variance)	**2,010.8 (A)**

Summary of variances

	£
Labour mix variance	327 (F)
Labour output/yield variance	2,011 (A)
Labour efficiency variance	**1,684 (A)**

(c) *Memorandum*

To: Finance director
From: Management accountant
Date: 10 September

LABOUR MIX AND OUTPUT/YIELD VARIANCES

The analysis of the labour efficiency variance into mix and output (yield) variances shows that there was a small saving in the cost of labour mix from using a slightly smaller proportion of skilled labour and a slightly larger proportion of semi-skilled labour. However, this was offset by a large adverse output (yield) variance as both grades of labour operated at well below the standard level of efficiency.

The variances could imply that semi-skilled labour is doing some of the work normally done by skilled labour.

Generally, variance analysis does not provide the answers but helps to pinpoint the areas where investigation is necessary and where questions should be asked.

The additional analysis provides little extra information compared with the efficiency variances. However, as little extra cost is involved to calculate the additional variances, it is probably worthwhile.